more
dream homes

100 inspirational interiors

more
dream homes
100 inspirational interiors

Andreas von Einsiedel

Johanna Thornycroft

MERRELL
LONDON · NEW YORK

For Orlando, Gwendolen and Robin

contents

contemporary 73–85

opulent 86–100

More Dream Homes, like its forerunner, *Dream Homes*, showcases 100 inspiring homes created by some of the most talented architects, designers, decorators, artists, antiques dealers and gifted amateurs. Homes of various types are featured, many of them innovative and exciting in their approach to decoration. Interior designers and decorators continue to shape the trends that inspire our choice of colours and furnishings, as well as the ways in which we use space and light in our homes and solve our storage problems, but the early years of the twenty-first century have heralded a greater desire for eclecticism than ever before.

Stripped of all period features, white, pared-down spaces that echo the utilitarian values of the 1920s and 1930s have been used to demonstrate personal taste in myriad ways. Twentieth-century furniture, lighting, carpets and fabrics – from the understated elegance of 1940s French design to the pop art of the 1960s – have become a great trend, but in interior decoration it seems that no single style really dominates. Many designers would admit to being influenced by the past, if only by the recent past, as well as having an eye on current and future trends, and architecture, of course, has an important part to play in the treatment of interiors. The individual who commissions the interior design of a modern house or a modern refurbishment of an old property, however, will be driven by various influences, not always the most obvious. No matter whether the choice of decoration is described as 'traditional' or 'modern', there will always be an element of modern style inherent in its creation, unless, of course, the owner or designer attempts a truly historic re-creation. Bathrooms and kitchens, larger and more luxurious than ever before, are treated as living spaces rather than mere utility rooms, and are by their very nature contemporary even if cloaked in 'period style'. Within the simplest of architectural spaces can be found a modern take on Victoriana or a contemporary version of Baroque; equally, fine period interiors complete with complex decorative mouldings, cornices, skirting boards, niches and pillars admirably suit modern art and contemporary furniture. The key is generally white or at least pale, neutral backgrounds devoid of pattern, against which 'anything goes' – although some things go better than others. Two examples of this style of home are nos. 5 and 76.

The 'English country-house look', the most copied style in the world, was created largely by the partnership of Sybil Colefax and John Fowler in the first half of the twentieth century, and later that of Fowler and Nancy Lancaster. This post-World War II invention changed the public's concept of what a country house should be. 'A room must be essentially comfortable, not only to the body, but to the eye,' said Fowler. 'The decorations must be mannered, yet casual and unselfconscious.'

Fowler's championing of cotton and linen for curtains and upholstery, rather than sombre velvets and machine-made tapestry, and his willingness to strip away centuries of brown varnish and to use pottery instead of porcelain, produced a style that became deeply etched in the public mind and set the benchmark for 'good taste' (see no. 95 by Colefax & Fowler and no. 94 by Graham Carr, who was an assistant to John Fowler). Such paint companies as Farrow & Ball and Papers and Paints (in the UK), Ralph Lauren and The Gryphin Company (in the US), Beckers (Sweden) and Auro Organic Paints (Germany) produced hugely popular ranges of historic colours and numerous shades of white, which continue to be combined architecturally in a single scheme in the layered Fowler tradition. Curtain treatments may now be less elaborate, and chintz used sparingly, but millions of decorative schemes produced today are based on the warm colours, deep, down-filled sofas, symmetrical arrangements of pictures and practical placing of table lamps that Fowler favoured. Our desire for comfortable, sociable, practical and elegant homes is universal, even though taste can vary greatly.

Every so often a seismic shift occurs in interior fashions. The 'feature wall' of the 1960s has reappeared in the first decade of the twenty-first century as a solid block of contrasting, sometimes clashing, colour. A single living-room wall is covered in vivid overscaled floral or geometric wallpaper and photographic images enlarged (although the Canadian Rockies are no longer popular) to be used as wallpaper. The 'feature' armchair has arrived, and the company Squint covers old furniture with vintage fabrics, to popular acclaim. Traditional fireplaces have been replaced with 'hole-in-the-wall' pebble-lined gas fires, and media rooms are now more important than dining-rooms. Early to mid-twentieth-century designs that were once the preserve and passion of architects and modernists have become mainstream, and original or reproduction furniture, lighting and rugs from the 1930s to the 1970s are now important elements of the modern interior. The work of such designers as Charles and Ray Eames, Fritz Hansen, Arne Jacobsen, Le Corbusier, Borge Mogensen, Verner Panton and Eero Saarinen – the list runs to many hundreds – have become 'must-have' pieces. At the same time, eclecticism has moved from a simple mix of antique and modern to one that is much less clearly delineated, and pieces from as late as the 1970s are now used alongside contemporary work. Egg and Butterfly chairs are paired with new works by such designers as Marcel Wanders, Philippe Starck and Piet Boon. The demise of 'brown' furniture looked set to continue, but, as fashion constantly repeats itself, a new generation, particularly in North America, have started to buy fine eighteenth-century mahogany furniture wherever they can find it.

Most of us find our own style and means of self-expression somewhere between the classic and the strictly minimalist. If any design object provides an expression of certain values, we choose it to enhance our own pleasure as much as to impress others with a statement about taste, modernity, value or knowledge. How we embellish our homes reveals more about us than do the clothes we wear, the car we drive or even where we live.

Some would argue that the tendency towards a 'global modern' style is reducing architecture and interior design to a characterless international look devoid of regional influences. Greater wealth and mobility – and, as a result, the creation of numerous 'designer' hotels – have certainly had an enormous impact on domestic interior design, and it is becoming increasingly difficult to identify the 'nationality' of a house or flat. Exteriors, of course, have a lasting impact on the look and feel of a country; the interiors are private, only seen by the public if they are deemed interesting or fashionable enough to be published. *Country Life* magazine in the UK and *Town and Country* in the US celebrate the work of many architects who build houses that respect not only the landscape in which they stand but also the history of that landscape, and *More Dream Homes* illustrates the diversity of interior decoration. It would seem that, although a distinct risk, the blandness of internationalism has not yet overcome the sheer variety of personal taste to be found across the world.

The relentless desire for new technology and a growing awareness that the resources needed to fuel our lives are increasingly threatened mean that we must all play a part in improving the sustainability of our homes. The facts are alarming. A large proportion of carbon emissions come from fuel used for heating, and demand for electricity is outstripping supply, as is the need for water. Fortunately, politicians in many countries are becoming aware of the urgency to find alternative, sustainable resources, and numerous awareness campaigns are beginning to make headway.

How we live really can make a difference, and there is plenty of choice in the market for furniture and fittings for the home. Simple solutions include changing to a condensing boiler, using low-energy lighting and energy-rated electrical equipment, choosing eco-friendly mineral paints, turning the heating down a little and the air conditioning off, installing double glazing and insulating the walls and roof. Anything made of timber should be from a renewable supply source. Where the organic food movement has led, enlightened fabric producers have followed: organically grown cotton and linen are now widely available. Importantly, however, we all need to reduce, repair, recycle and reupholster as well. As people move home more and more frequently, the wastage factor rises alarmingly. Brand-new kitchens are ripped out for reasons of fashion or personal preference. Thousands of metres of granite, marble and stone worktops are dumped each year. Larger baths and power showers and more of them per property mean an ever-greater need for vast amounts of water. It would not be practical to advocate a return to the grim days of a weekly bath, but professional and amateur designers and decorators are beginning to consider how much energy every new or refurbished home is designed to consume. Architects are learning, without diminished creativity, from the traditional techniques employed before our dependence on fossil fuels.

No matter how complex the challenges of declining space and energy sources, we will continue to be stimulated and surprised by the vast number of creative forces that produce new fabrics, furniture, colours, lighting, carpets and art with which to decorate our homes. It is hoped that *More Dream Homes* will provide inspiration and ideas for the decoration of any kind of home, whatever the budget, as well as delighting the eye.

classic 1–30

1 Less is more

Gleaming white inside and out, this historic house on the island of Nantucket, with its classic clapboard exterior, is a wonderful example of a restoration project carried out with the utmost sensitivity to time and place. Strict architectural guidelines dictated the manner in which the house could be subtly updated, and they allowed the staircase to be moved from the back to the front hall and an open-plan kitchen to be created at the rear. The floorboards were stained black to provide a strong anchor for the many other black tones and textures used in the interior. Granite worktops in the kitchen, lacquered furniture, picture frames, a pair of black leather chairs and pretty black tole wall lights add an attractive graphic feel to the rooms, but there is none of the coldness associated with some black-and-white schemes. Natural textured rugs soften the floors, and limpid blue–green colours used for upholstery and lamp bases echo the seaside beyond. All-white interiors tend to be associated with modern architecture, but as this house and no. 82 demonstrate, by way of very different architectural styles, monochrome period interiors have a beauty all their own.

classic

classic

2 Light and space

Characterized by high ceilings, period mouldings and a classic bay window, this London flat is one of several units converted from a large Victorian house. More recently, additional changes have been made to the layout of the rooms to maximize light and space. The main entrance now opens into a hall, the wall of which has been removed to create a framed arch through which the whole of the living-room is visible. Two more doors lead off the cupboard-lined hall into the living-room, and the dead space at the end of the hall has been filled with bookshelves. The bedroom door has been sited to line up with a door opposite – another device that enhances the feeling of space. Using the same natural-coloured timber for skirtings, doors and frames gives the scheme coherence, and the natural theme is followed through in the white roman blinds, simple linen curtains and seagrass matting. The original Victorian fireplace has received a contemporary makeover, and instead of grouping furniture around it, the owner has placed a pair of modern daybeds either side of a glass-topped table, effectively dividing the room into two zones.

classic

3 Perfect proportions

A traditional terraced house in the Notting Hill area of London has been modernized to incorporate the key requirements of modern living, including plenty of light and a sense of 'flow' between the spaces. Without making enormous structural changes, it is possible to transform the atmosphere of a house or flat by removing out-of-date woodwork and bathroom fittings, for example, and by simply replacing doors with square-arched open doorways, which can be made wider and taller than the original openings. This property had the potential to become exactly what the owner wanted, and it included a garden that he knew could be modernized along with the house. A new bathroom with limestone floors and sliding glass doors was installed. Opening the kitchen to the entrance hall dramatically improved the sense of space and light. In the kitchen, old cupboard doors were replaced with maple-wood doors, and new work surfaces were put in. Decorating every room in the same colour proved to be another good space enhancer. Black-and-white photographs are carefully grouped on the white walls, and dark Asian furniture is mixed with the honey tones of Biedermeier, while tan leather ensures a clean, contemporary look.

classic

classic

4 Cool Cape

The steeply sloping hillsides of Cape Town provide some of the most spectacular views imaginable. Seen from Table Mountain, the city spreads out in a panorama comprising the docks, leafy suburbs, far-stretching beaches and wine-growing lands, and penetrating beyond into the vast expanse of the Atlantic Ocean. Small, brightly painted houses, some dating from the eighteenth century, are clustered above the redeveloped port, an area with dwellings that are now keenly sought-after by those seeking a place in the winter sun. Although it had been improved by earlier owners, this two-storey house — with bedrooms on the ground floor and living spaces and a terrace on the upper level — needed further work. Two friends, both London designers, collaborated on the project. Building a pool where there had been just a terrace was the most difficult aspect of the work, but eventually it was possible to step out of the master bedroom straight into the water. Interior decoration was kept simple and spare, and all the furniture and fabrics were bought in Cape Town. African textiles and colourful wire baskets have been used to enliven rooms painted off-white and cream. Quirky touches include paper wall lights modelled on the heads of game animals.

classic

5 Classic tradition

The sheer beauty of this recently restored 1780s house in London is breathtaking. Trained in fine art, ceramics and furniture-making, the man who designed these interiors for his wife and himself has become a highly respected architectural designer who specializes in bespoke, fine-quality finishes, technological innovation and superb classical detailing. The house had been used as offices and a dental laboratory. Apart from the staircase, little had survived the ravages of the twentieth century. Panelling, architraves, doors, windows and skirting boards all had to be replaced, but the original shutters were found stacked in a cupboard ready to be restored and rehung. On each of the six floors, plaster mouldings and chimneypieces were replaced. Limestone floors, brown and bleached oak floorboards, Lutron lighting and the latest kitchen technology have been installed. The owner designed all the cabinetry and most of the furniture; his preference is for a few large-scale pieces based on period designs mixed with, perhaps, architectural fragments or fine antiques and vintage fittings in a rigorously pared-down style. This exemplary project won the UK 'Designer of the Year' award in 2005 for best classical residential interior.

classic

classic

6 Attention to detail

One great advantage of working with leading interior designers is that they have a wide-ranging knowledge about where to buy anything you might want for your home. In this large family house in central London, the rooms are luxuriously spacious and light, but most impressive are the carefully chosen mixture of modern and antique pieces, the harmony of shapes and textures, and the sheer quality of the detailing, including beautiful handmade curtains and blinds. The bedrooms are worthy of a five-star hotel, and in all the living areas a great effort has been made to create an ambience that suits the way the space is used. Works by some of the top names in the world of interiors are in evidence. The Emily Todhunter collection of furniture and lamps is complemented by fabrics from Abbott and Boyd, Nicole Fabre, Rubelli and de Le Cuona. Elements that could not easily be found, from furniture to hand-painted wallpaper, were specially designed and made. By choosing an intense red fabric for the walls of the home cinema, combined with fine carpet, velvet and suede, the designer has created a cocoon that encourages relaxation. As shown here, the best interiors combine luxury with practicality while allowing the owners to express their individuality.

classic

classic

7 Tailored chic

This vast flat occupies the top four floors of a Portland stone-fronted landmark building in London. With an area of 506 square metres (5447 square feet), it is bigger than most of the city's houses. A lift was installed during a major refurbishment, making the vertical living space practical and comfortable. Consisting of five bedroom suites, two large terraces, a cinema, leisure room and conservatory, the accommodation has been fitted out in elegant contemporary fashion. The colour palette is restrained, dominated by caramel, cream, off-white, chocolate and grey, with occasional red detailing. Visual interest comes from the varying tones and grains of such fine woods as wenge and walnut. Luxurious materials such as leather and suede, high-gloss lacquered surfaces and striated marbles and stone add textural contrast. Each room features electrically operated, tailored roman blinds made in plain or subtly striped linens; the bedrooms have custom-fitted wardrobes. In the drawing-room, a pair of antique console tables either side of the fireplace and two overscaled sofas are beautifully balanced by a pair of extended armchairs at the opposite end of the room.

classic

8 Studied calm

Interior designers are responsible for a lot more than simply choosing colours, furniture and fabric. At the centre of a constantly changing world that seeks to balance the requirements of comfort, style and function, they influence the way in which we all live, work and relax. Herself an interior designer, the owner of this London house trained at the Inchbald School of Design, which is renowned for producing graduates of impressive technical ability. She lived in the house for a while before moving out and beginning work on it. Efficient storage was a high priority, based on the need to instil a sense of calm and order into a busy family home. The owner designed a modern layout with the emphasis on informal entertaining on the ground floor and private retreats above. Scale and materials have been very carefully considered. Cupboards and shelving stretch up to the ceiling, providing extra space and good clean lines. All the floors and the four corner shelving units in the living-room are made of the same timber. To avoid having too much solid wood, she used wood-framed doors lined with linen fabric and double plantation shutters in the bathroom. Furniture is a chic mix of modern classics from Cappellini to Christian Liagre.

classic

classic

9 Understated elegance

Not long ago this former farmhouse in Provence was no more than a rundown stone cottage with several small agricultural sheds attached, all standing on a 1.6-hectare (4-acre) site. Luckily, the next-door neighbour became interested in the property and asked some friends of his, restorers and designers based in Aix-en-Provence, to draw up plans to redevelop it as a guest house. The project went ahead and the original property is now unrecognizable. Complying with the strict local planning regulations, the restoration experts have created a dream home. Specialists in regional architecture and pioneers of a new Provençal interior style, they have used fine polished stone and natural oak boards for the floors and kept the plastered walls plain white. Red is the accent colour inside and out. Simple printed and striped cottons characterize most rooms, but a grander gesture has been made in the main living-room in the design of a large, armless, back-to-back sofa upholstered in a woven fabric with an overscaled pattern. Moroccan reed mats soften the floors, and unlined fine-linen curtains shade the bedrooms. Iron tables and lamps, African pieces and beautifully crafted bathrooms and kitchen all add to the sense of quiet, understated luxury.

classic

10 Felt perfect

A closer look at this flat on two floors of a Georgian house in London reveals how the couple who own it have incorporated their possessions and style in complete harmony. For example, accessories made of felt sit happily beside carefully chosen antiques. A traditional material in Finland, felt has been brought to a wide public by one of the owners, who makes exquisite, sculptural and useful objects in brightly coloured felts. The key to the success of this interior-design scheme was to keep the background of each room very simple. The architecture of the Georgian period produced large, light and airy spaces; painting them white not only conveys a Scandinavian feel, familiar to the owner, but also allows all the items of furniture and accessories to be appreciated for their individual form and beauty. It was the Modernist architect and designer Erno Goldfinger who said: 'My furniture is made for human use and not to go with the room for which it is designed.' Although one owner believes in the romance and importance of memories associated with certain objects and the other prefers absolute minimalism, respect for each other's tastes has made it possible to combine their passions.

classic

classic

11 Orderly elegance

Even if the decoration in the main rooms of a home is cool and calm, halls and corridors are often well suited to intense colour. The owner of this London flat bought it from her interior-designer daughter, and, although the property was in good condition, she wanted to change its character to reflect more of her own personality. Apart from being the heart of the home, the kitchen would be used regularly for entertaining, and it was decided to remodel it in the style of a kitchen in Norway, with soft colours, white-painted chairs with gingham seat covers, and tongue-and-groove panelling. Warm coral and terracotta fabrics add colour to the bedroom and living-room, both of which have creamy backgrounds. Beautifully hung groups of pictures – even in the bathroom, where there is a gallery-like display of photographs – create a sense of order and interest in every room. Deep, down-filled chairs and sofas and plenty of soft cushions foster a completely relaxing environment. To make the most of the tall windows, curtains have been tied back very high, allowing plenty of light into the flat. There are table lamps in all the right places and a fine understanding of the importance of scale, exemplified by the decision to take the bookshelves up to ceiling height.

classic

12 Inside out

When one member of a couple longs for vibrant colour and the other insists on calm neutrals, an interior designer must find a compromise. A substantial makeover was required to bring this four-bedroom London house up to scratch. The designer delighted in the fact that the project would include the demolition of a back extension, allowing a new glazed-roofed dining-room and play area to be built. Her clients also wanted custom-made fittings and unusual pieces to be included in the plan. The house was totally refurbished. Underfloor heating was installed along with new bathrooms and a kitchen, and the garden was redesigned to complement the calm, contemporary interiors. While neutrals were agreed on for the floors and walls, the wife's passion for colour was not ignored. Indeed, colour has been added in all sorts of clever ways: through paintings, accents of red and orange, aqua-painted walls in the bathroom and the choice of dark wooden furniture against the pale wooden floors. William Yeoward supplied a wonderful chandelier and some of the fabrics. Craftsman Nick Allen devised storage solutions throughout the house, including making cedar-lined walnut wardrobes for the dressing-room. Compromise does not have to be bland.

classic

classic

13 Connoisseurs' choice

A beautiful view over a privately owned communal garden is a sought-after feature in a London property. This large split-level flat had the added advantage of its own private garden and roof terrace. Completely redeveloped and redesigned with few restrictions on budget and in a classic contemporary style, the apartment is now a spectacular living space. The use of fine materials is evident throughout. American oak flooring has been installed in the reception room that links the staircase to the entertaining areas and bedrooms. Known for her use of unusual marble, the designer chose an almost black stone for the floor and walls of the master bathroom, the effect of which is dramatic but not overbearing; a pair of glass basins and the clear-glass shower screens ensure that the space remains bright and airy. Entire walls in the bedrooms are taken up by custom-made cupboards, and there are also specially designed headboards, side tables and various styles of upholstered seating. There is a good mixture of vintage and contemporary detailing, and the well-thought-out lighting systems offer plenty of opportunities for changing the mood according to the circumstances or time of day.

classic

classic

14   Island life

Location is often as important as great architecture or interior design in defining a dream home. Take, for example, a private plot of land on the Caribbean island of St Lucia, set on a hilltop overlooking the ocean, add an inspired design for a living space, and a dream can easily be fulfilled. Reminiscent of Bermudan architecture, this house – as white as icing sugar – features a central living space with three sets of oval-topped doors front and back; off it, linked by walled walkways, are four identical pavilions projecting at angles to maximize the sea views. An open terrace sweeps across the front of the house, while a more sheltered outdoor living and dining space has been created at right angles to the living-room. The roof structure in the living area is exposed, increasing the feeling of airiness, and in true island tradition the bedroom ceilings are matchboarded (covered with tongue-and-groove panelling). Glass bricks are ideal for an external shower wall; the figured marble tiles echo the bricks in size and shape. Pale blue and navy blue are traditional seaside colours, used here sparingly but adding interest to the otherwise all-white scheme. Hinged shutters control the admission of light and, importantly, the flow of air through the house.

classic

15 **Perfectly preserved**

Many dream homes are characterized by a match between the owner's taste in furniture and artworks and the date and architecture of the building. This beautifully preserved and restored Georgian terraced house was built in 1776. Virtually all the contents were made before that date. The owners, an American and a New Zealander, are dealers in seventeenth- and eighteenth-century English country furniture, and the property serves as a showroom as well as an elegant, atmospheric home. The house had escaped many twentieth-century 'improvements', retaining much of its original panelling as well as shutters, doors with their latches and hinges, windows and fireplaces. Most importantly, the layout had not changed – no walls had been knocked down and the staircase was intact. All the rooms have been painted in muted tones of off-white, grey and green. There is little requirement for more colour since the range of tones and grains, as well as the patina of age, seen in furniture made of ash, elm, oak and walnut creates an effect that is singularly vibrant and textural. Fine country furniture in pale, uncluttered rooms can appear ravishingly sculptural and surprisingly contemporary.

classic

16 Mayfair magic

A broad entrance hall with a white marble floor is the first sign of luxury in this flat in London's Mayfair. The contrasting black border and gleaming walnut skirtings, architraves and panelled doors against white walls establish a strong modern look, which is emphasized by a pair of boxy console tables and tall upholstered chairs ranged against one wall. The double doors to the reception rooms can be left open when required to give a greater sense of space. As the property needed a complete refurbishment, the designer was able to choose many different materials to update each room. She made lavish use of beautifully figured marbles for the bathrooms, each of them different but treated in a spa-like manner. The kitchen is a modern classic in grey and stainless steel anchored by polished limestone flooring. A square living area is treated as a single space, with an enormous dark-wood coffee table and large patterned rug as the focal points, but the provision of a number of small tables of differing shapes and heights and a good mix of lighting make the room a very social space. Further elements of luxury include a separate dining-room and a media room – essential in flats of this quality.

classic

classic

17 Vintage and modern

Door panels incorporating swirling leaded shapes and stained glass are typically Edwardian features of this terraced house in London, but inside an altogether different atmosphere prevails. While the owners adore combining vintage and modern objects, they also like to add their own touches to create an individual look. A double reception room, formerly two rooms, is anchored by dark walnut floors and a pair of French chandeliers, and above each fireplace is an identical vertical mirror. Instead of buying period chimneypieces, the owners decided to leave the fireplaces barely adorned; strips of old embossed tin shelf serve as simple mantelpieces, and strings of lights are used to give a warm feel to the fireboxes. The house is painted in several shades of white, with slatted American-style shutters providing both privacy and good natural light. Broad horizontal, hand-painted stripes are a clever way to introduce interest to a child's room without over-elaboration. Individual decorative touches are to be found on lampshades, picture frames and chests of drawers; beads, lace, old buttons and feathers add to the quirky sense of fun.

classic

18 Palatial proportions

Spanning the width of three nineteenth-century houses, this London flat
is home to a high-powered professional couple who do a great deal of
travelling. They commissioned a well-known designer who produces
her own range of furniture and lighting to create interiors that would
incorporate old and new, English comfort and elegance, and more than
a touch of Art Deco glamour. The rooms in the apartment are very large,
so attention to scale was vital. In the living-room, walls lined in watery-
green silk form the backdrop to a mixture of wide sofas, comfortable
armchairs and plenty of tables, all anchored by the expanse of a softly
coloured Ziegler rug. Artworks, most of them large, are a prominent
feature of the flat. Eighteenth-century scenes of the Thames, abstract
works by Menez, a Serge Poliakoff and a Dutch old master make a
striking impact. Any good designer understands the importance of
mirror glass, especially where room proportions are awkward or there
is a shortage of light. In this case, mirror panels combined with painted
scenes make the dining-room a magic space. In the bedrooms, comfort
and glamour abound: silks, faux ostrich skin, rock crystal and silver
provide some of the many touches of luxury.

classic

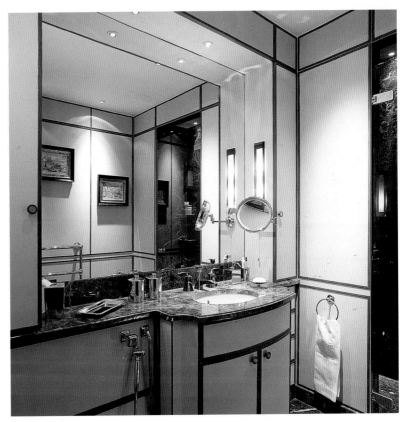

classic

19 On target

Occupying the ground and lower-ground floors of an old building in central London, this split-level flat has an interior that epitomizes bold and confident design. Well-known for her original work on a diverse range of projects, the designer gave careful consideration to making the best use of space. A good architectural eye ensured that the balance of scale and proportion was carried through from the living-room, where the tall bay windows remained intact, to the wall of very large storage cupboards in the bedroom. It was an inspired idea to make the bedroom door the same as one of the cupboard doors, creating a seamless and integrated look. Light was brought into the lower level of the flat by adding doors to the rear exterior wall and building a glass roof over what had formerly been a narrow strip of patio. A skylight at right-angles to the dining space lights the galley kitchen. The boundary of the lower-level space was pushed underground, and a large seating area was formed by placing upholstered, mattress-like cushions on a solid base. Finishes and furnishings are all sleek and contemporary.

classic

20 Pied-à-terre in Paris

The design and decoration of a second home or a city pied-à-terre are treated by some as an exercise in complete simplicity, requiring none of the usual detailing or finishes seen in a main residence. The Provence-based designer and owner of this small ground-floor flat in Paris took the opposite view. Facing the magnificent courtyard of a grand former *hôtel particulier*, these rooms were originally stables, comprising only walls and doors. The plan was to transform them into a venue for meeting clients and for overnight or weekend visits to the capital. French windows were installed on the courtyard side of the building, and the space was divided to form a large living- and dining-room, an exquisite oak fitted kitchen and, beyond, a roof-lit bathroom accessible from the bedroom. The great success of this design is the white-painted panelling throughout; some sections are mirror-panelled to reflect light from the doors. Red linen, cotton and silk are used for curtains and cushions, while a classic red-and-white toile fabric lines the bathroom walls. No scaling-down took place, which is why this small flat looks, and indeed is, much grander and certainly far more comfortable than its size would seem to allow.

classic

classic

21 | Design ingenuity

High ceilings and tall, well-proportioned windows were the features that attracted the present owner, a designer and stylist, to this ground-floor London flat. She transformed what had been two reception rooms into a comfortable home consisting of a combined living and dining area, a bedroom, a bathroom and a practical kitchen. The keys to her success were good planning and well-designed storage. A tall unit was fitted to one side of the bay window, comprising open shelving, cupboards and drawers. Rather than building a galley kitchen along a wall of the living-room, she created space for a kitchen between the bedroom and living area, including in the design an open arched entrance. A false wall was extended across the width of the flat, incorporating more storage space, a display shelf and the door to the bedroom and ensuite bathroom. Woodwork, walls, floors and the dining table and chairs are painted white. The curtains are of white calico, while large mirrors and mirror panels increase the sense of space and light. The furniture, a mixture of traditional and modern, is upholstered in pastel linen and white cotton. The pale-lilac bedroom and bathroom are luxurious and feminine.

classic

22 Young urban

As the pace at which we live and work continues to quicken, we put increasing demands on the people who design our homes. The prime requirement is a comfortable, warm, relaxing living space that functions efficiently and has plenty of natural light. The contemporary home must incorporate areas for entertaining and working as well as private areas, and for many of us, keeping up with the latest fashions in interior design is also a priority. Where elaborate curtains and carpets were once important, in the early twenty-first century the emphasis is on high-quality finishes and a multiplicity of textures, rare or exotic materials, and the creation of apparently seamless spaces where everything has a place. This three-bedroom flat in central London has been fitted out and furnished to meet these rigorous standards. Sleek and uncluttered, it contains all the high-tech appliances one might expect. Luxurious features include immaculate polished-hardwood floors, dressing-rooms, a super-modern kitchen and designer furniture mixed with one-off commissioned pieces. This is an example of a classic modern interior that with minimal updating will continue to look good for many years.

classic

23 Quiet quality

Part of a terrace of houses in London's Belgravia built in the 1820s
by the master-builder Thomas Cubitt, this third- and fourth-floor flat
stretches over a luxurious 240 square metres (2583 square feet). A
good-sized entrance hall with walnut flooring and a useful console table
sets the scene. The dual-aspect living-room was large enough to allow
the designer to group two overscaled sofas and club chairs around an
exceptionally large coffee table, while a pair of custom-made Macassar
ebony units flanks the central window. The choice of a low, round side
table and, on it, a tall, bulbous glass lamp has prevented the room from
looking excessively rectilinear. Attention to detail is evident in the use
of such sensuous fabrics as linen, silk chenille and leather. A circular
dining table has been coupled with curved, sleek leather chairs to
pleasing effect, and traditional cornices and fireplaces have been
reinstated. The three bedroom suites, all uncompromisingly modern,
include cashmere curtains, vintage furniture and suede-lined
cupboards. Needless to say, the most technologically advanced lighting,
audiovisual, security and air-conditioning systems have been installed.

classic

classic

24 Keep it simple

The modern desire for free-flowing, open-plan living spaces has created the greatest change in the way people decorate their flats and houses. In homes where the physical divisions between cooking, eating and living areas have been removed, one decorative approach is to have as little demarcation, by way of flooring materials or paint colours, as possible. In this terraced house in west London, what would once have been a neat front parlour is now home to a high-tech Boffi kitchen. Walls have been replaced by structural columns, so that the living area, probably the original dining-room, is completely open to the entrance hall, staircase and kitchen. A glass-roofed conservatory dining-room has been built over the side access to the rear garden. The whole ground floor has been treated as a single space. The walls are painted cream and there are no rugs to break up the pale floors. A Perspex coffee table is barely visible in front of a fireplace. Slatted timber shutters give the street-facing kitchen some privacy but, crucially, allow plenty of light into the house. The upstairs bedrooms and bathrooms also seem to be flooded with light, an effect that has been enhanced by the use of the minimum number of different materials.

classic

25 Two halves

The extension and modernization of this old house, the cellars of which date from the 1490s, was a challenge for all those involved. Now, with the work completed, the welcoming front entrance leads into an elegant, old-fashioned hall, but through a door to the right, beyond the study, is an altogether different world. An enormous glass-walled living-room has been added along the length of one side of the house. Linked to this magnificent room by a new terrace is a back extension accommodating a large new kitchen. Below ground level, and entered by means of a modern staircase from the living-room, is a series of open-plan spaces lit by a glass roof; one wall, clad in steel, is continuously washed by a gentle waterfall that shimmers in the low light. Through the glass-walled extension is an ancient brick boundary wall, making a wonderful contrast with the bright, contemporary interiors, which have been furnished by a young London designer in different shades of white, cream and red. Pale oak floors and white walls provide the background against which a marvellous mix of antique and twentieth-century furniture is grouped in several seating areas. The first-floor bedrooms and bathrooms are luxurious and warm, but decorated with restraint.

classic

26   Above the shop

When one is in the fortunate position of owning a four-storey house in
a city and of being able to dedicate the lower two floors to a work area
while using the other two floors as a living space, the idea of working
from home becomes much more appealing. Built in the 1740s, this tall
brick house in east London has been carefully restored with the aim
of preserving or reinstating as much period detail as possible. After
stripping off many layers of paint, removing crumbling plaster from
the walls and replacing the floorboards, the owner learned of a local
historical precedent for covering part of the walls in tongue-and-groove
panelling, so this is what has been done in many rooms. Although it
may be a poor man's substitute for oak, tongue-and-groove panelling
is nonetheless charming in its effect. Walls painted a soft vanilla-white
make the spaces feel warm, and fresh flowers add to the impression of
summer in the city. More reminiscent of a cottage than a town house,
the decorative touches signal country living. Lime-green, duck-egg-blue
and daffodil-yellow along with flower-print curtains and artworks by
Robert Clarke banish any trace of urban gloom.

classic

27 Federal revival

Upstate New York has some of America's most interesting surviving Georgian houses, many of which lay neglected until their rediscovery in the late twentieth century by writers, artists and antiques dealers, sparking a great revival of interest in the architecture of the Georgian period. Bought in a ruinous state a few years ago, this 1790s house with Greek revival additions was exactly what its most recent resident, an owner of antiques shops in New York City and a nearby town, was looking for. Unusually for both the period and the location, the house is built of brick rather than timber. Although the addition of partitions in the 1950s had created a warren of rooms, much of the period detailing had survived; windows, floors and fireplaces were repaired and the rooms' original proportions revealed. There is a harmonious mix of antique and mid-twentieth-century furniture, textiles and works of art. Since the house is set in a private wooded garden, the living-room windows have been left curtainless to make the most of the light, while painting the walls pale green has created a subtle link with the garden.

classic

classic

28 Georgian gem

This architecturally important Georgian house in central London, dating from the 1760s, had been badly neglected – to the point where its basement was derelict – when it was rescued by an artist, also a skilled designer and colourist, who painstakingly brought it back to life. Once the basement had been restored and new floor tiles laid, a country-style kitchen with space for two large dining tables and Suffolk Ball and Bar chairs was created. Several old dressers were filled with antique jugs and plates collected by the owner and his wife. He painted the stripes on the living-room walls by hand, making a fitting background to some of the Biedermeier furniture owned by the couple. A Gothic theme was chosen for the library; the fireplace, mirror and bookcases were all designed by the owner, who chose colours typical of the mid-nineteenth-century Gothic revival. Old Aubusson-style rugs, faded and subtle, suit these rooms perfectly. The dining-room panelling, which is painted grey-mauve, is original, as are the shutters and columns. The secretaire, sofa and chairs are mid-nineteenth-century Biedermeier, while the pretty octagonal table is English Regency. A Venetian mirror reflects light from the tall, uncurtained windows. It is always a joy to see a large house of this period so beautifully restored as a family home.

classic

29 Artistic triumph

An art collection can make a significant design statement; rather like an important carpet or rare architectural detailing, art can be taken as the prompt for a decorative scheme or the arrangement of furniture, as in this example. With a front façade that is typically Victorian, this house opens up to the rear garden in an entirely modern manner to accommodate the kitchen, dining area and relaxed living space. While the wall on to the garden is largely glass, the long party walls were ideal for hanging large works of art by Carlos Vergara and Antonio Guerrero. In the drawing-room, a picture by Daniel Senise creates a powerful focal point for the grouping of furniture. Paintings and black-and-white photographs are seen in all the rooms, and sculptures are prominent – most notably a group of small bronzes by Guillem Nadal. Fine rugs, both old and new, add colour and texture to the polished oak floors. There is an excellent mixture of contemporary and antique furniture, in classic combinations arranged for comfort. A number of pieces in the house were designed by the owner's brother, a Lisbon-based designer, who also advised on fabrics, special wall finishes and the remodelling of the bathrooms.

classic

classic

30 Designer at home

Structurally, this spacious flat overlooking the Rhine in Germany was in good condition when it was acquired by an interior designer, but it had last been decorated in the 1970s. At 260 square metres (2800 square feet) and on the first floor of a house built in 1901, it was a perfect space for the designer to transform into a home for himself. Original elements were preserved, including the tiled kitchen floor, the many sets of tall double doors linking the rooms, and the slim painted beams, which create interest and shadow on the high ceilings. Different tones of white are key to the decorative effect; the palest cream was used in the entrance hall, changing gradually to light stone as one moves through the enfilade of rooms. Seagrass matting provides a neutral background for the owner's contemporary and antique furniture, which includes Biedermeier pieces, a Lincolnshire (England) settle, a Dutch oriental chest and, in the dining-room, a French iron-and-timber table grouped with modern Spanish leather chairs. Striking modern photographs and pictures are prominent in every room, except for the kitchen, where two German posters of 1915 hang above the settle. The objects in this comfortable flat are carefully arranged and stimulating in their variety.

classic

eclectic 31–49

31 Balmy Balearics

What at first appears to be a traditional country residence is actually a typical town house on the Spanish island of Mallorca, restored by two German designers. The house is solid and square, with no entrance hall, so that the front door opens straight on to the street. The surviving rough stone walls and structural timber beams dictated the way in which the owners chose to decorate and furnish the house. The furniture consists of a charming mixture of rustic tables and chairs, comfortable modern sofas, a crystal chandelier and casual striped flat-weave rugs. Traditionally small windows with shutters meant that there was no need for curtains, but plenty of hard-wearing white denim was used for bed curtains and upholstery. Two terraces – one at ground level, the other on the roof – are treated as outdoor living- and dining-rooms and have been adorned with locally made pots and Mediterranean plants. Wherever possible, the owners have used only local materials and, being designers, have taken great care to respect the vernacular architecture, an attitude that enhances the joy of living in a historic and aesthetically pleasing environment.

eclectic

eclectic

32 Primary colour

Tucked away in a private courtyard in London's Chelsea, this exuberant home was formerly part of a 1980s development of purpose-built offices. During the conversion of the offices to residential units, the developer decided that she could transform part of the building into an ideal property for herself. Having bought the space she wished to occupy, she had the inspired idea of installing an internal curved screen of glass bricks to create a subtle division between the dining area and the kitchen. Glass bricks, popular since the 1930s, are most often used in place of conventional brick walls as a way of bringing light into entrance halls or staircases. In addition to the glass wall, other graceful curving and curling shapes define the look of these highly distinctive interiors, along with a collection of paintings by the English artist Mark Wigan. The strong primary colours of Wigan's work inspired the owner's choice of upholstery fabrics, cushions and vividly coloured and patterned kilims. Apart from the walls and kitchen units, almost everything – from the staircase to the breakfast bar in wrought iron and glass, the candelabra, the chairs and tables – features soft curves, scrolls and gentle organic shapes. Pale stone-coloured floors and grey kitchen units are a classic combination, and there is a good mixture of task and mood lighting throughout.

eclectic

33 English eccentric

For lovers of mid-eighteenth-century English architecture, this Wiltshire property is the dream home. With a walled garden, a coach house and a wild garden large enough to keep chickens, pigs (as the owners do) or perhaps a horse, it is a house that stirs the emotions. The interiors were created largely by the present owner's father, who painted the brown-toned design on to the walls of the first-floor landing and hung original William Morris wallpaper (dating from about 1910) in the small sitting-room. All the furniture, except a Rose Tarlow sofa, is well-worn and chintz-covered or cushioned with antique fabrics, many bought at country-house sales. The table in the hall was made on site by fitting a seventeenth-century oak top on to new legs. The dining-room, formerly the kitchen, retains a massive original fireplace, which would have been used for cooking. Each room has a display of paintings and prints, from Piranesi and Raphael to family portraits and photography by Angus McBean. Spanning the width of the dining-room wall is a framed nineteenth-century Tapa (bark) cloth from the Pacific. This wonderful family home has been created by different generations with no desire to change anything, and in it one is barely aware of the twenty-first century.

eclectic

34 Ancient and modern

A London-based architect and her husband set out to find a holiday home that was only a short flight, or indeed a train journey, away from Britain. They wanted a place that was easy to maintain and had good access to restaurants but was close enough to countryside for summer walking and exploring. Prepared to restore an old property herself, the architect chose an ancient town house in the centre of St-Rémy-de-Provence, a medieval walled settlement famous for, among other things, the fact that Vincent van Gogh had been incarcerated in the local asylum. During restoration, Roman culverts were discovered below the floors. Unusually, the house is detached from those on either side of it, so is likely to be much older than its neighbours. The sense of age is greatest at entrance level, which features stone walls and a curved arch leading to a dimly lit space, probably used as a wine cellar or workshop in the past but now serving as a cool reception room. Off it rises an old stone staircase leading to two bedrooms on the first floor. On the second floor are the kitchen and living-room, which has been modernized by the addition of a series of folding windows across the front wall. Decoration is simple and contemporary; the furnishings are a good mix of old and new.

35 Material benefits

Appearances can be deceptive. This English house was built in the 1950s in the style of the early twentieth century. The current owner, an artist and garden designer, saw through the building's years of neglect and its lack of interesting architectural detail to realize that it offered huge scope for improvement. Some surviving oak detailing on the exterior coupled with the owner's love of barns inspired a major refurbishment, which centred on the construction of a two-bay, two-storey oak-framed extension and dining conservatory designed by the owner herself. Using green oak for the construction and red bricks and Chinese slate for the floors has created a sense of solidity and permanence. The house is now full of textural interest and, above all, wonderful natural light. As much glass as possible has been used, particularly in the new first-floor bedroom; glass panels were set into the roof, and windows and doors were inserted on three sides of the room including the fireplace wall. Painted a warm ochre, the living areas appear to be bathed in sunlight. The same colour was used for the retaining walls of the terraced garden, establishing a clever link between the interior and exterior spaces.

eclectic

eclectic

36 The collector

Occupying an upper floor of a brick-built Georgian house in London's Hampstead is a light-filled flat owned and designed by a well-known collector of and dealer in antique textiles. It has a drawing-room with space for dining and a tiny, well-organized kitchen. A set of double doors leads to the main bedroom, and beyond the kitchen is a further bedroom and a bathroom. The furniture and decorative objects span many centuries and cultures, from pre-Columbian to the 1950s, Africa to Italy, and Uzbekistan to Indonesia, and each item is an example of fine craftsmanship. The owner has found some ingenious ways to store her extraordinary collections. She sleeps on top of a plan chest, the drawers of which are filled with embroidery, silks and antique pashmina shawls. The waxed-pine floorboards are softened by tiny Tibetan rugs in an indigo-and-ivory chequerboard pattern, and on the walls is a constantly changing feast of vivid and rare panels, textile fragments or dowry and marriage pieces. The furniture ranges from Chinese antiques to Ethiopian chairs and Shaker designs of the 1950s. Everything has been chosen because it is handmade, or because it is a fine example of its type, or because it delights the owner's eye.

eclectic

37 Fifties sketchbook

From the outside, this brick-built twentieth-century house in northern Germany looks conventional enough, but the interior decoration is highly individual. After improving the layout of the rooms, the owners decided on a 1950s-inspired colour scheme, which changed the character of the house entirely. In the 1950s, the decorative use of apple-greens, yellow, raspberry, sage and aqua became a popular way of demonstrating that colour could, and should, be fun; brown was banished for many years. The key to the success of this retro style is a fresh, summery mix of flat-painted walls and solid blocks of colour. While some of the items of furniture, such as the dining chairs bought when an old barber's shop closed, are original designs from the 1950s, the look does not rely on period pieces alone. In the timber-beamed living area, furniture was chosen by shape and, apart from a sofa upholstered in a loosely floral fabric from Designers Guild, everything from the yellow leather club chair to the pink linen wingback is resolutely plain. A single pink-spotted rug breaks up the flow of polished beechwood floors, while the first-floor bedrooms are colour-coordinated to create warm and relaxing spaces.

eclectic

eclectic

38 White is right

No matter how many new fashions emerge in the world of wall colours, paper panels or exotic timber finishes, white remains a perennial favourite among owners and interior decorators; there is hardly a paint company today that does not offer a range of 'whites' – historic, bright, tinted, warm or cool. For the artist owner of this London house, Farrow & Ball provided the many different tones of white and grey she sought to reflect her and her husband's largely French provincial tastes. Both of them visited antiques fairs from a young age, and they share a love of French and Italian furnishings: lamps, lights and wall sconces as well as fabrics. This luminous background, including white floors, boldly sets off everything in the house, more so than would be the case with any other colour apart from black. Colour is introduced by means of a constantly changing selection of the owner's own work (much of which is inspired by the house itself) and that of a number of British painters, including Ivon Hitchens, Mary Fedden and Roger Hilton. The choice of picture frames varies from plain black to gilded and painted mouldings, and the arrangement of the work reflects the owner's keen eye for display.

eclectic

39 Object lesson

This flat is the London base of one of Britain's most acclaimed interior designers, who has been variously described as cultured, erudite and never afraid of colour. His work shows evidence of numerous influences and cross-cultural styles, but it is always grounded by discipline and form – books, for instance, are carefully ordered by subject matter – as well as original design. The pine-panelled living-room in this flat features a group of loose-covered chairs upholstered in the designer's own abstract 'Japanese' fabric. The blue-and-red rug is echoed by the Mark Francis painting that hangs above the fireplace and by the collection of ceramics – some antique and some by Picasso – that lines the painted shelves. Several striking carved-wood mirror frames were designed by the owner as well as various side tables called J.S. Drum and J.S. Cloud. He has a rare and enviable ability to bring together harmoniously seemingly disparate styles and colours. Purists might say that the colours clash and the range of artwork is too diverse – but that is the whole point. There is nothing more restrictive than too much good taste.

eclectic

40 Shared passion

Long-established villages in rural France have a charm all their own. Part of the attraction of such settlements lies in the fact that so many of the old houses remain unrestored, allowing new owners – in this case, a Danish designer of film sets and interiors and his Scottish wife, also an interior designer – to realize their own vision of a perfect home. Close to the vineyards and chateaux of Bordeaux, this classic house, built between 1640 and the mid-nineteenth century, has two distinct faces. The front overlooks the market square, while the rear has glorious, uninterrupted views of the countryside. Many of the original elements – fireplaces, shutters, floors and panelling – have been preserved and renovated. The generous proportions of the building give enough space for four large bedrooms and four bathrooms. White paint throughout, together with the many metres of John England Irish linen used for curtains and upholstery, creates a light and soothing background for an eclectic mix of furniture, ranging from antiques and old pictures to pieces from Ikea. A wonderfully original idea is the decorative use of numerous wine boxes, with their labels attached, lining the kitchen walls. The large scale of the dark metal lanterns and chandeliers works particularly well against the high, white ceilings.

eclectic

41 Scale and drama

Choosing to leave structural brickwork in its raw state is in itself a bold design decision, but in this case the owners have amplified the drama by leaving the first-floor beams exposed and creating as open-plan a design as possible. The old bricks are unevenly but beautifully coloured and full of character, unlike modern machine-made bricks. Tiled floors in all but the raised dining area look appropriate and provide an easy-to-maintain surface. Key elements of the design include the overscaled timber-framed windows and full-height doorways and the partial walls at the entrance to the kitchen and beside the simple wood-and-metal staircase. The choice of large, moody artworks in every room adds to the resonance of the place, as does the quirky mixture of modern and antique furniture. Shape and texture play a greater role than colour and pattern in this flat, although an oriental rug in muted, rusty reds defines and softens the main seating area without looking out of place. Brick walls in a bathroom seem an ideal choice – the combination of rough and smooth textures is particularly pleasing – and lining a bedroom wall with mirror glass adds glamour while increasing the light and sense of space.

eclectic

42 Designer in residence

A split-level artist's studio might not generally be regarded as an ideal place to live, but here is an example of a property whose owner, a designer, has devised some ingenious solutions to a specific spatial challenge. Two important ingredients of his success were the immense height of the ceilings and the fact that the studio had plenty of good natural light from a wall of windows facing north over a park. The first thing that had to be done was to create a sleeping gallery in what was formerly the artist's canvas storage area. Through a curved archway beside the staircase is a compact kitchen, screened by harlequin-painted doors and lined with shelving containing cookware, china and glass. The owner's drawing board has been set up in a space under the sleeping gallery. While every square centimetre of room has been utilized, there is an abiding impression that this is a large flat. The trick is in the detail. A crystal chandelier, overscaled artworks, fine antiques, large lamps and a proper fireplace combine to produce a certain grandeur – unusual in what was formerly no more than a work space.

eclectic

43 Personal space

This flat near the River Alster in Hamburg bears witness to its owner's knowledge of design influences spanning several centuries. Now a decorator and shop proprietor, the owner once studied painting, and she has been inspired in addition by artefacts in museums and art galleries. In this instance, she took on a neglected flat with few obvious attractions apart from its spaciousness and wonderful windows. She added such period detailing as plaster mouldings and timber panelling and embarked on painting each room in her favourite 'late summer' colours. By removing most of the wall between two reception rooms, she was able to create a winter garden, which not only gave views over the Alster but also made both reception rooms much lighter than they had been. Relatively small structural changes can have a great impact on the sense of 'flow' in a living space, and where rooms are lit by windows at both ends the quality of illumination is greatly improved. The owner has furnished her flat with a mixture of flea-market finds, Gustavian and Baroque furniture, contemporary lighting of her own design and a collection of overscaled stone lamps.

eclectic

eclectic

44 Eastern influence

There is a delightful simplicity about this small London house, but it has no lack of practical or indeed comfortable spaces. Although the owner is a designer, there are no fashion statements; the interior design caters entirely to the owner's need to house her books, sleep peacefully, cook efficiently and read, write or entertain in comfort. She was an early Western enthusiast for Chinese country furniture and has continued to furnish her houses over the years with a group of favourite tables, chairs, stools and boxes. The dark, rich tones of Huanghuali and elm are set against John Oliver's 'Casablanca' white paint, blue linen and the red accents of textiles, old quilts or lacquered objects. A pair of mah-jong tables is used for dining, singly or placed together. The many sculptural chairs are often arranged to make an original room divider. On the first floor there are three bedrooms, all decorated in the same combination of blue, red and white. Each room features a different style of bed: a curvy Italian metalwork antique, a traditional Indonesian bed, and a daybed upholstered in blue and white. The wooden floors are completely bare and, apart from a single large painting by Gerald Kelly, the living-room walls are pristine white.

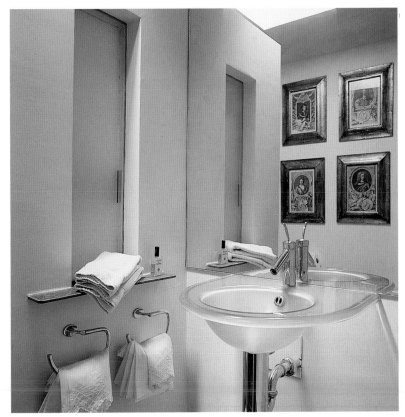

45 Paint perfect

Subtle paint finishes are key to the sense of elegance that permeates this town house in Chelsea, London. Muted wall colours include off-whites, putty and yellow, and woodwork is treated with a pale French grey throughout. This decorative approach creates an important link with the furniture, especially in the dining-room, where an antique painted chest of drawers, dining table and chairs all feature a similarly distressed paint finish. The classic combination of white and blue, from pastel to indigo, has been used in many of the rooms. The kitchen curtains are in a bold blue-and-white check fabric. Paler blues are evident in the bathroom and bedroom coupled with intense blue prints and plains to add impact. The dining chairs have circular blue-and-white seat pads, which tie in with a large antique painted panel that has been fitted behind the chest of drawers. Although the rooms are not particularly large, the owner, an interior designer, likes to work with fewer large pieces of furniture rather than numerous small items.

eclectic

eclectic

46 Flower power

Childhood memories and a love of sunshine and flowers inspired the choice of colours and fabrics in the restoration of this clapboard house in Connecticut as a vacation home. All the woodwork in the welcoming kitchen, dominated by a large fireplace, has been painted a strong Mediterranean blue – a colour echoed in the blue-and-white plates hanging on the white walls above. The perfect complement to blue is yellow, introduced into this interior by means of a large painting by Roger Muhl. Identifying pastels as her particular favourite for fabrics, the owner, a designer and writer on lifestyle subjects, has chosen a flower-patterned pink, blue and white chintz for the living-room sofas. White walls and bare floorboards add a light and summery touch to the decorative theme, and the owner's choice of country chairs and tables suits the cottage architecture perfectly. In the master bedroom upstairs, flower paintings, fresh garden flowers and quilts featuring flowers blend surprisingly well with the pink, yellow and green floral bed hangings. The key to the success of the interior design is in the choice of complementary pastel colours.

eclectic

47 Luminous glamour

Creating a light-filled interior involves a great deal more than simply using lashings of white paint, as is demonstrated by this London family home, which is owned by a famous designer of handbags and shoes, beauty products, jewellery, perfume and bedlinen. A lover of 1950s glamour, the owner has mixed colours, textiles and patterns in idiosyncratic ways that are free of the 'designer interior' stamp. Each room has been treated individually. The entrance hall is lined with Chinese handpainted wallpaper; the lilac-and-white dining-room has a mirror that amplifies the glitter effect from crystal and Perspex objects; and the drawing-room is furnished with richly coloured pieces spanning more than a century. Red roses are a prominent feature of the owner's work, and for her bedroom she chose a red carpet and a red velvet bedcover, both of which make a good foil for the patterned wallpaper. Many of the interior fittings were designed for the house, including the silver-painted Jali radiator screens, the bedroom armoires and some of the carpets. While intensely personal, these rooms are glamorous but timeless and, above all, full of luminosity.

eclectic

48 Paris original

A beautifully restored eighteenth-century house on the Ile St Louis in Paris would be many people's idea of a perfect home in the city. The artist who lives here today has been in residence for several decades. She is not a collector as such but says that many of the most exotic items in the house 'were just picked up wherever we went'. Tall French windows, white walls, white rugs and a white bedcover provide the simplest of backdrops to a fascinating, imaginative interior that has evolved rather than been designed. The contents are of great personal interest or evocative of past experiences dating back to childhood; some of the most important are associated with travel, Venice or close friends. This is undoubtedly a French interior, one that is characterized by whimsy and diversity, individuality, improvisation and a sense of humour. It would be impossible to find its contents in ordinary shops. The owner exemplifies a typically Parisian insouciance in her adoption of a style of living that cannot be taught and is hard to copy.

eclectic

49 Entertaining priority

When the owner of this London house, a man of many talents, decided that a new look was required for the much-loved home he had occupied for more than twenty years, he had two priorities. As a successful restaurant entrepreneur, he needed a space where he could cook and entertain to his heart's desire, and he wanted to do it amid 1940s-style glamour. The largest part of the project consisted of removing the rear wall in order to install a modern conservatory, thereby creating a strong link with the garden, which had been designed by Stephen Woodhams. The new, open-plan space incorporated a large dining table as well as a professionally fitted kitchen. Cherry wood was chosen for the units to echo the furnishings in the adjoining rooms, which include a formal dining-room at the front of the house. Featuring a glass-topped table with curly gilt legs, a mid-twentieth-century portrait above the fireplace, and a pair of very tall, narrow mirrors either side of the chimney breast, the living-room has a genuine 1940s feel; a club armchair in this room is typical of the period. Not all houses could be adapted so successfully to satisfy their owner's desires.

eclectic

country 50–72

50 Defying fashion

When this old family home in England passed to a younger generation, it was inevitable that changes would be made. The house, built about 1820, was taken in hand by a woman who not only is an experienced designer but also deals in antique and twentieth-century furniture. The interior design and decoration were reviewed, and consideration was given to improving the layout and proportions of the rooms. A plan was devised to build a substantial extension to house a new drawing-room on the ground floor with bedrooms and bathrooms above. Simplifying and opening up the kitchen meant removing an old butler's pantry and a staircase, but the extra space and light has proved a great bonus. New windows were chosen to harmonize with the old, and, where possible, reclaimed materials have been used, including flagstones for the linking hall; door handles, taps, basins and radiators are all period pieces. A set of antique doors opens into the drawing-room, and the floorboards were cut from old beams. The owners like understated eighteenth-century Continental furniture, rich detailing and fine fabrics set against soft, organic paintwork; tall gilt mirrors make a strong vertical statement. This house displays confident English design at its very best.

51 Barnstorm

The sculptural quality of the numerous old oak beams in this former barn was one of the things that attracted the present owner into what she describes as an impulse purchase. Located in rural south-west France, the barn and its adjoining house required three years' restoration work before the owner could move in. The property has a traditional exterior of stone walls and light-blue shutters, but the interiors are markedly different. The kitchen area, once a cattle stall, has the appearance of a weightless white construction that seems barely to touch the timber framework. It is contemporary and practical, designed in such a way that diners cannot see over the countertops to the work area beyond. Set under the rafters in the old hayloft, the master bedroom overlooks the main living area. The subtly varying tones of the timber create a soothing ambience that is kept quiet and calm by the choice of leather furniture, cream and white fabrics and old stone. Very little colour was needed in such a strongly defined architectural space.

52 Country comfort

Although varied in terms of architecture and size, English country houses are generally associated with expectations of warmth, comfort, informality and pleasure. The smaller examples of the style, especially if they are typically Georgian in design, have become increasingly popular and expensive, and few have survived unaltered. Built not by the aristocracy but by, for example, members of the clergy, successful farmers or tradesmen, they work as well today, in terms of proportion, light and layout, as they did when they were built. The London-based couple who own this mid-seventeenth-century house in the West Country were not concerned that changes had been made to the property, first in the eighteenth century and again in 1820. They decided that, apart from renewing the roof and windows, they would subject the house to a sensitive and minimal refurbishment. For example, unless disfigured by flaking paint, the walls were left undisturbed. Wallpaper was preserved or copied, existing paint colours were matched and fabrics were chosen to suit the owners' collection of antique furniture. Even the bathrooms, which are new, are pleasingly old-fashioned in style.

53 Gothic folly

The English fashion in the eighteenth and early nineteenth centuries for building parkland follies has led to some intriguing twentieth-century conversions. Designed as hunting lodges, bath-houses or picnic pavilions, follies were frequently set in sublime landscapes. This Gothic example was rebuilt and restored as a weekend retreat by a London-based dealer in old masters and his friend, an interior designer. By using salvaged materials, moving the staircase, replacing the doors and windows and changing the floor levels, the owners achieved a more practical use of the space. The paint colours on the walls – warm yellows, buff and red – set off a collection of blue-and-white Chinese plates and lamps. The furniture and pictures, a mixture of equestrian subjects, botanical studies and landscapes, were chosen to complement the architecture. Chippendale-style chairs flanking an octagonal dining table, gilt-framed mirrors, small chests and a writing desk all look perfectly at home in the space. The bedrooms are curtained with archive-print fabrics simply hung from poles. Many of the windows have been left bare; there are no neighbours, and the expansive views are one of the main attractions of a folly.

54 Island refuge

The vernacular architecture of Mallorca is characterized by thick rubble-stone walls, small wood-framed windows and plenty of shady, covered seating and dining areas – features that help explain the island's huge appeal to second-home owners. The climate is good, and until recently there were plenty of old farmhouses there that were ripe for restoration by northern Europeans seeking a place in the sun. A German couple who run an interior-design business knew Mallorca well and decided to acquire a property on the island and create their perfect holiday refuge. The 200-year-old house they bought has been decorated and furnished in a more sophisticated style than would be typical of a simple farmstead, although many local details have been included. The stained-timber kitchen with its open shelving, stone worktops and clay pots is suitably rustic. Bedrooms are light and airy, and the shiny tiled floors are softened by cotton dhurries. In the dining-room a wonderful crystal chandelier has been hung low over the table, and one wall has been covered by a panel painted with a naïve scene. The loggia is furnished for dining with a pair of old painted console tables, an iron daybed and a summery table and chairs; an exotic painted panel links all the colours most effectively.

55 Gothic revival

Not put off by the daunting nature of the restoration work required, a young couple took on this substantial Victorian rectory and created a place of great beauty. Thirty people worked on the house for eighteen months. Fine Gothic stonework was revealed behind boarded-up walls, but it soon became clear that many additions had been made to an earlier building. Behind the façade lay the good proportions of a Georgian house. With no professional help, the owners – inspired by influences ranging from Classicism to the French designer Jacques Garcia – undertook the interior decoration themselves. The reception rooms are grouped around an inner staircase hall. Seen from the main entrance to the hall, the combined library and living-room is on the right, opening to a stone corner tower. Painted in colours of 'old rose' and white, the drawing-room occupies the second bay, and beyond it is the dining-room. These rooms are furnished with a mixture of antique furniture, fine fabrics, hand-blocked wallpaper and oriental rugs, as are eight bedroom suites, but on the rear ground floor the mood changes to contemporary for the more private spaces. Bulthaup supplied the kitchen, and solid blocks of wall colour set off the mostly modern furniture in the living-rooms opposite.

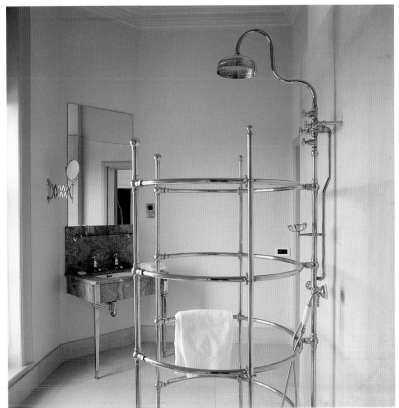

56 Treetop retreat

Living in a tree house might not be everyone's idea of bliss, but in the case of this owner it was a dream that began in childhood and has persisted all his life. A suitable, large pine tree was found in the grounds of his home in Provence, and discussions with a friend led to the drawing up of numerous designs for a variety of fantastic tree houses. It was a technically challenging task to build a light enough structure on a support that would not damage the host tree. In the event, an ingenious rubber-lined steel girth was devised to allow the slow expansion of the tree trunk over time. The house itself is reminiscent of a tiny colonial cottage constructed entirely from cedar. Glass-less windows are made of wood, and a small hole has been cut in the centre of each to allow air to circulate when the window is closed. Simple folding chairs and a timber bench provide seating, and a console table is fixed to one wall. There is an outdoor deck on which to sit while contemplating the landscape or anything else one might want to consider in this most private and captivating of retreats.

57 Art house

The artist owner of this eighteenth-century house in eastern England is a committed colourist who believes that white rooms are dull, both to paint in and to live in. Each room in the house may be painted in several tones of one colour, and the hue of the woodwork may differ from that of the walls, but the colours in a single room are always closely related to one another. These gentle, friendly rooms have been furnished with pieces collected over many years: some inherited, others bought at local salerooms. The effect of slowly adding favourite finds – a chair here, a side table there – makes it seem as if the rooms have evolved naturally over several generations. Closely grouped works of art are key to the success of the look. The kitchen is the most authentically rural space in the house, but there are plenty of other country-style elements, including large, comfortable beds, capacious chests of drawers, cosy rugs on the floors and pretty second-hand curtains at the windows. The house is used for a variety of purposes. As well as being a family home, it is both a painter's studio and a place where painting courses are run.

58 Retiring gracefully

Set on sloping ground below an ancient Provençal village was a small house with poky rooms but astounding views – and the potential to become a perfect year-round home for its new English owners. They realized that they could almost double the size of the residence by removing partition walls and expanding the outdoor living areas. In doing so, they have created an airy, spacious home well suited to the extremes of the local climate. The building is an L-shape, one wing of which houses a large living-room containing a monumental brick-lined fireplace. A small seating area near the entrance marks the boundary of the bedroom wing, which also contains the kitchen and dining-room. The covered veranda overlooking a newly built pool, grassy terraces and an olive grove has far-reaching views across the Luberon plain. Most of the furnishings came from the owners' previous home in England. White sofas and chairs are grouped on a limited-edition rug by Gillian Ayres; a collection of 1950s signed Daum glass and a magnificent 1940s Murano glass ceiling light add shimmer to the living-room; and a collection of artwork by Anne Pourny and Francesca Chandon brings vivid colour to the white-painted walls.

59 West Country character

This 500-year-old farmhouse with seventeenth- and eighteenth-century additions in south-west England was inherited by its owner when she was only twenty-three. It had not been modernized since 1911, when, among other improvements, the black-and-white tiled floor was installed in the master bathroom. The owner began the daunting task of restoration on a tiny budget by stripping hessian off the walls, exposing early dark oak panelling in a number of rooms. Since there were no inherited possessions, which can often dictate colour schemes or influence the styling of rooms, it was decided to give the house a light, neutral look using cream and stone-coloured paint, white fabrics and rustic furniture. Simplicity and functionality were also important because the house was destined to serve as a bed-and-breakfast business as well as a home. The kitchen was updated with units made from old doors and cupboards. Local stone – the same stone as that used in the old floors – was used for the new worktops. Inexpensive furniture and accessories were bought at auction and in France. The timeless combination of pale paint and a variety of woods in subtly different tones works as well in the country as it does in a modern flat.

60 Gallic style

Screened by old oak trees and flanked by an orchard of pears, plums and apples, this seventeenth-century former priory in Normandy was restored by its Francophile owner, an interior designer, in the best French tradition. Used as a farmhouse after the Revolution, the house is now reminiscent of a charming miniature eighteenth-century *manoir*. With little structural restoration required, it was a matter of transforming interiors decorated in a dull 1960s style into a restrained and elegant modern home. Hessian was stripped off the walls; the old brickwork was exposed in the dining-room and living-room; and all the flush doors were replaced with period panelled ones. Dados and Louis XIII mouldings were added, and Burgundy flags were reinstated on the ground floor. French style dictates that the grammar and vocabulary of architecture are important; aesthetics come before comfort, although there is more than a nod to cosiness and warmth. For this house, the furniture, mirrors and decorative objects were bought from Parisian auction houses, local *brocantes* and provincial antiques shops. Pale pink and yellow pigments were chosen for the walls, and curtains were made of simple checked linen or unlined calico.

61 White light

One of the challenges of taking on an unmodernized house is deciding how far to go in terms of restoration and refurbishment. This house in Sussex, built in the 1790s, was a sorry sight on first viewing, but the prospective buyer felt that it had enormous potential and went ahead with the purchase. Multiple layers of paint and varnish were slowly scraped back, revealing a great deal of original panelling, including cupboard doors, but the chimneypieces had been removed and the interior was extremely dark. In addition, the house had no heating and only rudimentary plumbing. The old-fashioned kitchen, with its Belfast sink and wooden worktops, was greatly improved by the addition of a pair of windows either side of the fireplace and by removing old ceiling boards. Tongue-and-groove wall panels and floors lend great charm and a sense of authenticity to an interior; in this case, they have been painted matt white, with the result that the space appears not only larger but also, critically, much lighter. Furnished with a mixture of antiques and junk-shop finds, old Irish linen, white china and stripped pine, the house feels light and airy but has not lost its unique character.

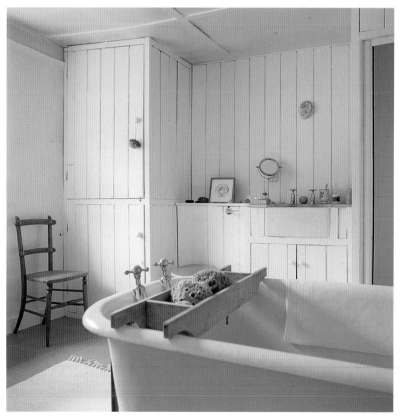

62   Reviving tradition

When the current owners first saw it, this eighteenth-century Provençal farmhouse appeared almost derelict. Modern partitions had been used to carve up the interiors into boxlike spaces, and it was hard to tell how the original house had been laid out. However, the owners, both designers, had plenty of experience of renovating old dwellings, and once all the superfluous layers had been removed, it was clear to them that they had acquired a gem. They planned to create a traditional French house – perhaps a little grander than a farmer might have aspired to, but one that would provide year-round comfort in a region of dramatic variations in seasonal temperatures. Warm, earthy colours were chosen to complement the terracotta floor tiles. Stone fireplaces, painted *trompe l'œil* panelling and faux-marble skirting boards were used to set the scene. Period detailing was emphasized throughout. Cupboard doors have been lined with pleated fabric; china is displayed on open shelving; and there is an eclectic mix of Swedish and French furniture. The kitchen splashback wall is lined with traditional glazed green-and-white tiles, while a hefty butcher's block makes a practical work surface. Printed cottons and closely grouped paintings all add to the Gallic country-house atmosphere.

63 Barn conversion

A photographer with a passion for the Arts and Crafts period and his wife, an acclaimed artist, have converted an 1840s stone barn in the English Cotswolds into a comfortable home entirely of their own design. The conversion respects the vernacular tradition of the area, and all the materials have been sourced and made up locally. Reclaimed Cotswold stone slabs were laid on the ground floor, wide English elm boards on the upper floors, and a mixture of elm and oak in the kitchen, bathrooms and bedrooms. Every fitting, from window latches to door furniture, and all the light fixtures were made especially for the house, as was all the wooden furniture. These intrepid builders even opened their own quarry to supply building stone. The walls incorporate traditional horsehair-and-lime plaster; the colours were mixed at home. Adrian Mustoe made the kitchen; Colin Hawkins was responsible for the lighting; and Colin Clark made much of the furniture. Inherited oriental rugs add dashes of colour, but little embellishment is required in this house, where wood and stone provide all the variety of colour and texture needed. The overall effect is not only beautiful but also totally in keeping with the building and its environment.

64 Magic Mallorca

A rural residence, especially in a country with a warm climate, can never be entirely divorced from its surrounding land or gardens. This is particularly true in Mallorca, where the old stone fincas (farmhouses) appear to have grown organically from the bedrock. Covered terraces are important living spaces; in this case, a series of broad stone arches creates the sense of an indoor room, but the space is breezy and full of light. Comfortable seating is provided in the shape of relaxed and manoeuvrable cane chairs. Chunky, close-set structural timber beams are the dominant feature in most of the rooms in the finca. Some people in Mallorca choose to treat their interiors in a strictly modern manner; others take a relaxed country approach to furnishing and decorating, mixing local antiques with French, English or Scandinavian furniture. Having established an interior-design and furnishing shop on the island, the owners had accumulated a great deal of knowledge about vernacular building styles, which they have successfully incorporated into their own home. With their pale sandstone floors and whitewashed walls, the rooms have been treated to a palette of natural colours, neutral linens, cotton tickings and the occasional print.

65 Cottage comfort

Many people who change their place of residence from the city to the country are in pursuit of a romantic dream, believing that they will find a better quality of life away from the urban jungle. Others move for professional reasons, to be in a more convenient or more congenial location – as was the case with the owners of this charming cottage. She is a design director for a large fabric house based outside London, and he is a photographer. They wanted a property in the most rural position possible and, when they found this house, decided that they were prepared to endure the three years of work that the project would require. With its low ceilings and colours ranging from pea green to lilac, and from terracotta to clotted cream, the cottage is characterized by rooms that exude warmth and a comfortable intimacy. Old floorboards are softened with colourful rugs or sisal matting, and a pale limestone floor has been laid in the kitchen. In some rooms, woollen blankets are used for curtains, with poles consisting of simple lengths of hazel. Furniture is mismatched in time-honoured country style, fresh flowers abound, and every surface is treated to collections and arrangements of jugs, hats, textiles or quirky objects prized for their shape or colour.

country

66 Basle beauty

Fine period detailing should be regarded as a bonus in any house, and the great thing about today's attitudes to design is that a host of different styles can be accommodated in an infinite variety of modern interiors. This elegant early nineteenth-century villa near Basle in Switzerland was decorated and furnished by a couple with a wide-ranging knowledge of European style. The most striking features of the house are the beautifully proportioned windows and the fine wood grains of the floors, architraves and doors. While the drawing-room has the appearance of an English country house, with its needlepoint rug, floral curtains and low tables piled with interesting books, the coral-coloured dining-room with its unusual painted table and chairs appears to be influenced by French and Swedish styles. Particularly effective are the symmetrical groups of pictures throughout the house, and the way in which a collection of majolica plates has been displayed on an old carved shelf unit in the dining area of the small kitchen. A beautiful example of what is usually called 'traditional' interior design, the house feels wonderfully orderly and secure and is a much-loved home.

67 Country continuity

With a house built in the seventeenth and eighteenth centuries, a horse stud and 810 hectares (2000 acres) of land, an English country estate such as this is one of the most prized pieces of property in the world. The well-proportioned rooms, wonderful windows, ancient floorboards and nooks and crannies that lend themselves to many different uses are the stuff of dreams. Unusually, all the windows in the house have been left free of curtains. Preferring natural illumination both during the day and at night, the owners have decided that shutters and white roller blinds are all that are necessary. Also unusual is the fact that the interior is painted in a range of different whites, from lime-white and gardenia to a pale mushroom. There are few sources of colour, apart from several rugs, the collection of oil paintings and jugs of fresh flowers. Waxed pine, polished mahogany and the varying colours of the wooden floors create a gentle continuity throughout the house, replacing rooms themed by colour, wallpaper or fabric. It is a modern look for a very old house, and an approach that has become extremely popular.

68 Budget beauty

The idea of moving to a lovely old house in France can be driven as much by a desire for increased space as by a quest for a complete change of lifestyle – as was the case with this pretty eighteenth-century house in the Lot-et-Garonne region. The young Anglo-American owner took on much of the restoration work herself, including creating a workshop where she designs and makes lampshades. The cheapest way of updating interiors is to paint them, and in old French houses white, pale blue, grey or muted greens work particularly well. Many original features of this house have survived, from the wobbly flagstone floors and wooden staircase to doors and windows and, of course, the irregular beams. Each room has a distinctive character. An abstract stencil pattern in red has been applied to one of the bedroom walls, creating an effect that is more casual than wallpaper; the red-and-white theme is taken up in headboards covered in floral fabric. A lovely antique crystal chandelier and a decorated curtain pelmet bring touches of grandeur to the dining-room. Inexpensive oriental rugs add colour and warmth to the floors, and comfortable old armchairs have simply had single pieces of fabric draped on the seats and large cushions filling the backs.

69 Keeper's Cottage

When a London-based American couple chanced on a Victorian cottage on a piece of land deep in the English countryside, the property had little to recommend it apart from a very private location. It did not even have a proper garden. However, the wife, an interior and garden designer, quickly realized that, though small, the house could easily be augmented and, crucially, an old garage could be converted into a guest lodge. She devised a plan to extend the cottage to create a kitchen and dining area with a master bedroom above it. Early on she designed and planted a new garden. More recently, a garden room has been added facing the stream that runs through the plot. The interior spaces have been skilfully reconfigured to create a spacious hall and a new staircase. Pretty oak windows were repaired or replaced and the old game larder was converted into a cloakroom. The choice of black-painted kitchen units and a black Aga cooker is simple and dramatic. As the cottage is often used as a vacation home in the winter, as well as the summer, it is important that the rooms are warm and cosy. The sofas are deep and the bedrooms are decorated in a modern country style, making this renovated cottage a wonderful place for entertaining friends and family.

country

70   Reinventing the past

Hidden behind modern buildings in the old part of a coastal town
in southern France, this eighteenth-century house has been treated
to a highly sensitive, almost invisible restoration, which began with
the demolition of nineteenth-century additions to reveal the original
structure. Its owner, an interior architect and designer, has a passion for
peeling paint, original finishes and period fittings. He added windows
for extra light and set about revealing the age-old wall colours, floor
tiles, doors and shutters. He essentially turned the house upside-down.
The ground floor now consists of an entrance hall and a spare room. The
first floor comprises a bedroom, a bathroom and a landing used as a
library; while the top floor, formerly a series of tiny rooms, has been
opened up to create the living, dining and kitchen areas. Local antiques
shops and *brocantes* provided most of the antique furniture, along with
rustic garden chairs, old 'foxed' mirrors and lighting. The only modern
piece is a comfortable sofa covered in old linen sheets. Apart from a
touch of blue–green in the kitchen and a red-and-white-striped cushion,
there is little colour in the house; decorative interest comes from the
textures and natural tones of wood, plaster and metal.

country

71 Holiday home

Finding the ideal holiday home can take a great deal of time and usually involves making a compromise between old and new – a compromise that, in this case, has been triumphantly achieved. The core of this now delightful residence on the island of Mallorca was a small farmhouse without running water or electricity, but the property had some land attached to it, wonderful views and plenty of potential. The new owners called on an interior designer who had worked with them on a previous home. A low-tech restoration was planned, encompassing the original small house, a right-angled addition and the conversion of two separate barns. One barn has become a guest house, the other an office. The new wing is barely distinguishable from the old; it appears to have evolved rather than to have been built deliberately. The use of traditional materials was an important feature. Beamed ceilings, whitewashed walls, old Mallorcan tiles and practical latticed wooden doors in the kitchen, along with small traditional windows and tiled floors, create a convincing sense of age. The interiors are simple, casual, pretty and summery, although the large fireplaces are often in use during the winter.

72   Mill house

Built in the mid-eighteenth century, this former flour-mill in Hampshire, England, was converted to residential use in the 1930s by an architect who was strongly influenced by the Arts and Crafts movement. Many of the handcrafted timber elements have survived and been enhanced by the current owners. After converting outbuildings to give themselves extra space, the couple, who are both designers, removed unwanted ceiling boards and partitions to expose supporting oak beams, thereby highlighting the building's rustic construction. Rather than imitating a country-cottage style or trying to create a coordinated interior, they chose furnishings that they love. Some pieces were inherited; others were designed and made by one of the owners. A pair of large Knole sofas was bought specially for the house, and artistic friends and local craftspeople made many of the pictures and ceramics. Colour was an important factor, since the abundance of wood in floors, ceiling beams and staircase could have felt overwhelming. The new white table and chairs look stylish under the timber-and-glass roof. House conversions can sometimes seem disjointed, but this harmonious example carries echoes of the building's working past while providing for modern living.

contemporary 73–85

73 Courtyard house

A small urban space that had formerly consisted of no more than run-down workshops, this site required radical creativity to produce a design for a modern family home. Fortunately, the prospective owner had the right credentials: she is an award-winning architect who was undaunted by the apparent difficulty of the project. After investing much time and thought, she produced sketch drawings of what she describes as a courtyard house or a mini Italianate villa. Now, with the project completed, a simple front door set into a brick wall is all that can be seen from the street. Inside, a staircase leads up to the planted courtyard, either side of which are the bedrooms and bathrooms. At the next level, the house opens into a pure white space containing the kitchen and dining-room and, above, the cube-shaped living-room. A rooftop garden floats above the living-room. The interiors are white and bright but enlivened by primary-colour accents. Upside-down living of this kind is gaining in popularity. After all, why live on the ground floor when the best light and views are at the top of most houses?

contemporary

74 Space saver

Very small flats offer a particular design challenge. As a former boat-builder, the owner of this flat – now a furniture and kitchen designer – was used to working with restricted spaces. In this instance, he bought part of a former industrial building that needed total reconfiguration. Essential to the project was the addition of two windows identical to the existing metal ones. The open-plan kitchen, dining and living area is unified by wooden floors and the simple outlines of the discreet kitchen units, a timber-clad island cube and a modern wooden dining table. Underfloor heating allows maximum use of wall space. The beautifully lit hall is actually a passage through several storage spaces including a cloakroom and an office, all screened by doors and sliding panels. An acid-etched panel allows light to filter from the wet-room, which is lined with Formica bonded on to marine plywood, into the rest of the interior. Evidence of the owner's joinery skills can be seen throughout the flat; in addition to the teak basin and all the beds, he made the floating walnut bench that is set along the fireplace wall. Luxurious grey velvet curtains cocoon the living area on cold nights.

contemporary

contemporary

75 Stress-free

Belgium, particularly Antwerp, is home to some of the world's most innovative architectural and design companies. A partner in one of those practices designed this flat for herself on the ground floor of a nineteenth-century house. The apartment, which covers an area of 360 square metres (3900 square feet), was originally made up of many small rooms, but the insertion of tall, square openings and opaque glass doors has given a much greater sense of spaciousness, creating vistas through the flat. Uniform grey-brown oak floorboards are complemented by textured walls painted white and grey. The rooms are large enough to allow broad linking areas and plenty of storage, two great luxuries in city dwellings. Narrow floor-to-ceiling radiators are sculptural and space-saving, leaving the void beneath the windows uncluttered. Low, upholstered seating has been set against the walls to make the most of what is already a large space. There are pleasing combinations of shapes and colours in every room – from the dining table in sycamore and steel, designed by the owner, to the blocky wooden chair by Gerrit Rietveld in the hall and the softly curved black-and-chrome living-room chairs by Gipsen. The flat is a stress-free refuge from the outside world.

76 American smooth

Space, light and height, those most desirable characteristics of modern interiors, can also be found in many period buildings, as seen in this flat in London's Belgravia. One of many designed by John Nash in the early nineteenth century, the house is typical of the style with its broad chimney breasts, good fire surrounds, well-proportioned windows and ceiling heights that correspond to the size of the rooms. The American designer commissioned to redecorate the flat was asked to focus on multiple textures – kidskin, cashmere, raw silk and wool – rather than colour, using a strictly limited palette of white and black combined with the rich hues of twentieth- and twenty-first-century brown-wood furniture. Pale wall-to-wall carpet and white paint throughout offer an appropriate backdrop to carefully chosen pieces of furniture and artworks. Distinctive items include tables by Jean-Michel Frank and Eileen Gray, a dining suite by Emile-Jacques Ruhlmann, a Jean Dunand screen, a chandelier by Verner Panton and table lamps by Paul Dupré-Lafon, along with such custom-made pieces by the designer as a pair of desks that double as side tables and several parchment-covered stacking tables. There is no pattern in the scheme. This is precise but instinctive interior decoration.

contemporary

contemporary

77 Bare essentials

All the hallmarks of a famous minimalist architect's work – including enlarged windows and overscaled doorways fitted with folding panelled doors – are evident in this London flat. The interiors have been stripped back to the basics, leaving behind none of the fussy Victorian detailing. The work had been carried out for a previous owner, but the flat presented a later purchaser with exactly the type of city base he wanted for his frequent visits to the capital. The flat's present look is the work of a designer who had undertaken previous, more complex projects for the owner, and is the result of a brief to furnish and equip all three floors in a very short time. The rooms are spectacularly spacious and lofty with some wonderful modern detailing, especially in the combined kitchen and dining-room, where a wall of bookshelves contains at its centre a cooking unit; the other appliances and the sink are housed in a simple marble slab set in front of tall windows. Paintings were chosen by the designer from a Royal College of Art degree show, and much of the furniture was sourced from the Conran Shop.

contemporary

78 Mountain retreat

Set in a pine forest high above the Cape coastline of South Africa is a house that has been designed to integrate entirely with its extraordinary surroundings. The exterior is reminiscent of a building by Frank Lloyd Wright, but there is far more glass than he would have used. The house was built as a retreat from a hectic business life in Johannesburg by a couple who are nature-lovers, walkers and keen observers of the local flora and fauna. Their interest in the natural world is reflected in the choice of building materials and in the interior decoration, which is dominated by the colours of sand, stone, driftwood and Table Mountain itself. The master bedroom fills the first floor, while the ground floor is devoted to open-plan living spaces and guest accommodation, flanked by stone terraces and an exquisite black, naturalistic swimming pool. The wife, a furniture designer and photographer, has designed a practical and sociable kitchen, including an industrial-scale, chilled, walk-in larder; entertaining is a high priority for the couple. Modern furniture is combined with pieces made of reclaimed timber. The checked cotton upholstery in the living-room has faded from black to tan in the powerful light.

79 Architectural practice

Rising through three levels and with a footprint of just 6 square metres (65 square feet), this former mews coach house has been brilliantly redesigned as a two-bedroom flat and architectural studio. Light was a vital consideration. The mews façade features a double-height oval-topped window with glazed doors at ground level echoing the former coaching doors. A pair of small circular windows is set either side of the oval at first-floor level, while a single round window on the rear wall fills the living area with pearly luminescence. Access to both floors is by means of a set of spiral steps projecting from a single column; the design is reminiscent of scaffolding. Locating the bathroom on the ground floor in a central 'pod' made it possible for the studio to be used independently of the private spaces above. Kitchen storage has been provided next to the pear-wood work area by filling the entire wall with a row of seamless cupboards. The choice of primary accent colours against white-painted walls lends a slightly 'retro' feel to the living area, in which chairs by Charles Eames and Ludwig Mies van der Rohe and tables by Eero Saarinen are anchored by a royal-blue Danish carpet.

80 Prime location

Extending over two floors of a period building in London's Mayfair, this flat is not only unusually spacious and highly practical but also full of luxurious touches. There is direct lift access to the upper floor, which consists of a living-room, a dining-room and a combined kitchen and breakfast room, together with a large roof terrace. The lower floor, containing three bedroom suites, is reached via a glass-and-steel staircase designed by Eva Jiricna. Stone, steel, glass and dark-stained woods create a strong backdrop for modern furniture. Where colour has been used, it makes a big impact, but the look of this flat relies on strong architectural elements, such as suspended ceilings, unframed glass doors, panelled walls and cutting-edge design. The Minotti kitchen is made of rare Macassar ebony topped with Zimbabwean marble. Heavy silks were used for upholstery and to dress a circular revolving bed. Bathrooms include steam-rooms, a freestanding oval bath and wenge cabinets. Wardrobes are framed in hardwood and lined with silk panels. The latest media equipment, heating and cooling systems, electronically controlled blinds and multi-mood lighting are also in evidence.

contemporary

contemporary

81 Design family

Owned by the proprietors of a landmark London shop selling the finest twentieth-century furniture, accessories and lighting, this old house has been designed and decorated in a very modern way to accommodate a family of five, including young children. When the shop opened in the 1960s, many of the great designers of the previous decades were virtually unknown in Britain. Now, the names of Le Corbusier, Bruno Mathieson, Eero Saarinen, Ludwig Mies van der Rohe and their contemporaries are familiar to many people, and collecting originals and re-editions of their work is no longer unusual. As the choice of furniture here shows, having a young family does not mean sacrificing design to function. In the kitchen, bright polycarbonate dining chairs by Philippe Starck are teamed with a circular breakfast table. The ribbed-glass-fronted storage units are stylish and practical; the floors are a mix of stone and timber. Curtains were thought too fussy, so American shutters were installed in the main rooms. The interiors are largely white, but shots of colour can be seen in floor rugs, upholstery fabric and bedcovers. Huge paper pendant lights are affordable and sculptural.

contemporary

82 Clever contrast

The continuing fashion for creating contemporary interiors in old houses produces some surprising results. This 300-year-old timber-framed house near Bonn in Germany appears untouched from the outside, but inside it has been transformed by a respected German designer who was asked to convert two houses into one and completely update the living space. The brief included highlighting the contrast between old and new. The designer opened up what is now the dining-room to link the two houses and designed a new staircase against what had been the shared wall. Some of the original casement windows have been kept, but the formerly boxy rooms are now open and airy, and structural columns have replaced loadbearing walls. The white-and-cream decoration is an ideal foil for ebonized furniture and black picture frames and lampshades; some of the original black ceiling beams have been left exposed, and the window frames have been picked out in black paint. Le Corbusier sofas, Chinese chairs and graphic modern art are mixed with Biedermeier antiques. Floors are kept pale by the use of white stone and white, textured rugs, and there are no ceiling lights; lamps are preferred for greater cosiness.

contemporary

83 Level living

To a young couple in search of an ultra-modern home in London, this flat in a converted industrial building seemed perfect, with its open-plan living area, guaranteed parking space and absence of staircase. The conversion and decoration of the flat had been completed before the couple bought it, but the style suited both the building and their own taste. The original pine floorboards in the living area and the exposed brickwork might be too rustic for some people, but the flat makes no apology for its past – the old metal-framed windows have been retained, for example – and, in fact, it offers a surprisingly neutral background for an interesting mix of furniture. A curvy Victorian sofa has been upholstered in plain cotton and a second sofa has been covered with dark-blue velvet. A pair of eighteenth-century-style chairs and a simple glass coffee table are practical but keep the space uncluttered. The kitchen features a Bulthaup System 20, which consists of timber-and-steel freestanding units that are ideal in a room without any period detailing. Reflecting the popularity of overscaled images, one wall of the living-room has been covered by a photograph of a large shop-window display.

84 London calling

A well-travelled international design consultant and his wife have transformed what was formerly a gloomy 1970s flat near Eaton Square in London into a light and airy living space. The project involved replacing the kitchen and bathrooms, painting all the rooms, restoring the parquet floors, and furnishing the flat with a harmonious mixture of antique and modern furniture. The couple collect a wide range of twentieth-century photography and have a particular interest in recycling objects that had a practical use. The coffee table was made by placing a sheet of heavy glass on top of two old jars filled with coffee beans. A twig-and-plaster French beehive on the table still smells of honey, and an old carved wooden door-latch from Botswana sits on the mantelpiece. While the living-room is warm and calm, with ivory walls, curtains and upholstery, the dining-room is altogether different. A large iron chandelier from Guinevere works well with a pair of iron candelabra on the floor. The walls above the wooden panelling were painted an unusual colour from the Ralph Lauren range, and a striking Zebra pattern by Andrew Martin was used to upholster the comfortable chairs; a glass tabletop is mounted on an olive-root base. In the study, a Le Corbusier sofa has been teamed with a modern side table and lamp.

85 Urban renewal

In many major cities there is little opportunity to design new housing, so young architects become highly skilled at transforming all types of building into contemporary living spaces. Old houses often have small rooms, each with a defined purpose, and these small rooms tend to be dark. This 1840s house once suffered from such drawbacks, but it has recently undergone a transformation. By removing the back wall and excavating part of the garden, one of the owners, an architect, was able to build a glass extension over two levels. From the front entrance, one can see straight through the property to the garden, while the alterations and clever use of glass have massively increased the sense of space. Although a more formal living-room exists on the first floor, the family spend most of their time in their 'light-box' and garden. The owners are ardent fans of mid-twentieth-century furniture, and have collected works by, among others, Hans Wegner and Serge Chermayeff, combining these clean-lined, craftsman-made pieces with handmade textiles.

contemporary

opulent 86–100

86 Country squire

Built in 1580 and fashionably updated in the eighteenth century, this mellow red-brick house in Suffolk is set in 28 hectares (70 acres) of parkland and gardens. Owned by a man who describes himself as a collector, dealer and designer, it has been restored with great care and patience. The stone-flagged entrance hall – a majestic space containing antique busts and an unusual oval marble-column table – sets the scene for a grandly furnished house that is nevertheless warm and welcoming. An inlaid opium bed has been adapted to create an impressive coffee table in the drawing-room, while a pair of overscaled plum-velvet sofas brings to the room a sense of English country-house comfort. Late Victorian baths have been re-enamelled but otherwise left untouched. A reclaimed-slate floor has been installed in the kitchen, and a magnificent handmade copper extractor hood stretches along the wall above the Aga cooker and cabinets. To make the most of the lightness of the interior, the colour scheme has been restricted to a palette of off-whites; the location is so private that window treatments are minimal. One of the twelve bedrooms is furnished with a bed made from very old panels and French barley-twist posts, creating a room evocative of the early nineteenth century, although every room in this elegant house continues to evolve.

opulent

87 Chester Square

Belgravia in central London is well-known for its mid-nineteenth-century white-stucco houses overlooking imposing garden squares. While some owners and designers have decorated these handsome residences in a pared-down, contemporary style, an American couple from Los Angeles asked an English designer who had refurbished several other properties for them to give their new home the traditional English treatment. This look has survived the vagaries of fashion, in part because people who have collected fine furniture, portraits, mirrors and porcelain from various periods want to have an appropriate historical stage on which to display them. Before the interior decoration could begin, a major refurbishment was carried out from the roof to the basement. Cole & Son supplied historic wallpapers, while most of the fabrics, copied from eighteenth- and nineteenth-century documents, came from Colefax & Fowler. By combining eighteenth-century chandeliers with mainly Regency furniture and modern sofas, the designer has interpreted the scale of the rooms to perfection. The careful placing of mirrors, portraits and small pictures provides an all-important vertical definition, but none of the rooms feels crowded or over-designed.

opulent

88 Brussels belle

This residence in Brussels, dating from about 1900, is typical of a particular kind of continental European town house that was conceived for living and entertaining on a grand scale. It is distinguished by perfectly proportioned ground- and first-floor rooms linked in some cases by full-height, mirror-panelled doors and with tall windows front and back. Marble steps lead to the staircase hall. The only big change that had to be made in updating the house was to bring the kitchen closer to the living areas. All the original interior-design elements are intact, and the owner, an artist, has enhanced every room with her collections of antiques, contemporary and period pictures and rugs, as well as examples of friends' work. The huge second-floor space is given over to a home studio where designs for textiles, paper products, tiles and paper dresses are created. The rooms are supremely flexible. Small dining tables are set up for intimate gatherings; seating can be rearranged to suit large or small groups; and the interiors literally shimmer from the effect of strategically placed mirrors. Layers of colour merge subtly with white-painted and panelled walls. Everything about this house has a painterly feel, and red is the linking colour in every room.

opulent

89 Added glamour

The American designer who transformed this grand London town house had been asked by his client to 'add glamour'. Before any decoration could begin, a major programme of structural work and updating was undertaken. Each of the five floors was redesigned, the layouts were improved, and emphasis was placed on maximizing light and areas for entertaining. The basement kitchen features bleached-oak units in Arts and Crafts style with limestone worktops. Next to the kitchen is a relaxed family living-room and conservatory dining area leading into the garden. A slightly more formal living-room and dining-room are found at ground-floor level. A wall of mirror glass has been used to expand the sense of space in the long, narrow dining area; a glass-topped table enhances the lightness of the room and undoubtedly increases the glamour factor. In fact, mirrors – antique and modern – played a large part in the scheme; every room sparkles in their reflection. The house accommodates an interesting mix of eighteenth- to late twentieth-century furniture and light fittings, bought during shopping trips in London and Paris, as well as pieces that were specially designed for the house.

opulent

90   Artful arrangement

Antiques dealers' homes are likely to reflect their stock in trade, as exemplified by this house in Arundel, West Sussex. A former coaching inn dating from the fifteenth century, it is characterized by an eclectic mix of English and French country furniture and accessories assembled from far and wide. The style is neither town nor country, but the deep sofas, abundance of tables and colourful fabrics put the emphasis on comfort and relaxation. The owners like their treasures to be displayed in a well-organized fashion: pairs are better than singles, and interesting and unusual groupings are created by teaming objects of contrasting size, shape and colour. Old exposed brickwork, ancient timber beams and tiled floors allow for a less rigid scheme than plastered and painted walls would have done. Not everything is antique, however. The dealer's eye for adapting lovely 'bits and pieces' has resulted in the production, for example, of coffee tables using decorative old ironwork. It takes confidence and skill to mix textiles, china, timber and furniture from different periods. Antiques have a way of fitting into almost any interior; it is the way in which they are combined and arranged that indicates twenty-first-century living.

91 Art inspired

As a developer of hotels, bars, restaurants and clubs, the owner of this central London flat had a clear vision about the refurbishment of his own home. His plan was to transform the conventionally designed maisonette into a large, open living space with floor-to-ceiling windows, glossy American black-walnut floors and a new staircase incorporating glass panels below a walnut handrail. The staircase has been made more of a focal point by the enlargement of a rooflight above it. Apart from a rich-red wall in the bathroom, the flat has been painted white, considered the best background for a collection of contemporary paintings. A large multicoloured work by Simon Rayne was the inspiration for the colours chosen for the L-shaped sofa and glamorous cushions. At right angles to it hangs a black-and-white photograph by Terry O'Neill. Seating in this area consists of a classic Ludwig Mies van der Rohe Barcelona sofa and a pair of Charles Eames chairs *c.* 1969. A sleek kitchen was created with gunmetal-grey units topped with stainless steel, creating a masculine, clubby feel. Red was also chosen for a curvy sofa in the bedroom; the flat-fronted clothes cupboards are upholstered in faux suede.

opulent

92 Pure Paris

This large flat overlooking the Place de la Bastille in Paris has been decorated in classic Parisian style. Polished parquet floors flow through the space; double doors open in succession to create long views; and each room is treated to a combination of vibrant painted decoration and contrasting styles of furniture. Decorative schemes were chosen for particular reasons. The blue-and-white room at the centre of the apartment was inspired by a Directoire mirror and furnished with French antiques; the sofa was upholstered in red silk. In the white oval drawing-room, the mood changes to cool and pale. Its traditional elements are complemented by a contemporary arrangement of nineteenth-century furniture combined with glass, metal and mirror glass, filmy organza and shiny satin fabric. In the bedroom, black walls provide a dramatic backdrop to gilt mirrors and picture frames, nineteenth-century antiques and white busts. The smallest of several living-rooms has been decorated with terracotta-coloured walls above a white dado, and mirror tiles have been used to increase the light; glossy 1940s furniture is an ideal choice for this room. The flat is filled with covetable objects but is arranged in a modern and comfortable way.

93 Continental style

Essentially a single large room – a small sleeping area combined with a living-room and a kitchen set against the hall wall – this Continental-style London flat is the creation of a designer and collector known for his ability to produce extraordinary interiors from the humblest beginnings. After stripping the space of partitions, false ceilings and carpets, the designer embarked on the business of decoration. Inspired by the film *The Third Man*, the decorative scheme was to be based on a variety of masterly paint effects that would transform the rooms from ordinary to opulent. A chalky faux-gesso finish in Naples yellow was applied to the walls of the high-ceilinged living-room. By painting the vaulted hallway in a realistic imitation stone-block and the bedroom a rich red, the owner set the scene for his intriguing collection of furniture, textiles, pictures and mirrors. He particularly likes using groups of chairs as a design tool; chairs can be moved about easily, and a versatile set means that, in a small house or flat, a dining table can be set in any space. The colour scheme in this flat is a classic blend of soft yellow, sage-green and grey enlivened by the use of bold red textiles.

opulent

94 Divine inspiration

An old schoolhouse in Dorset made an ideal canvas for a man who designs and paints furniture and is an advisor on colour and interior decoration. Interiors painted by artistically creative people always express a highly individual style. In this case, the owner was influenced by Chinese ceramics and holidays in India, and he not only decorated the walls with an overscaled 'tree of life' pattern but also made and painted furniture specially, including chairs, tables, shutters and a new chimneypiece based on a Batty Langley design. The wooden floor in the splendidly proportioned combined living- and dining-room is painted in a diamond trellis pattern, which imitates marble and wood. A rich-yellow paint was used for the lobby hall, and the main bedroom scheme was based on blue-and-white Kashmiri crewelwork curtains; a slightly different fabric covers the walls. In the guest bedroom, white walls set off the many tones of red; the bed hangings were a special order from Colefax & Fowler. The owner is also a collector: Aboriginal paintings, Uzbek textiles, a French chandelier and African masks have been successfully combined with carved Irish tables and needlework from Morocco. The house is a delight to all the senses.

opulent

95 English classic

An American couple relocating to London found a six-storey house in Belgravia that perfectly suited their needs. Beautiful period detailing had survived; French windows allowed plenty of light to illuminate the well-proportioned rooms; and there were wonderful garden views and space for staff. The decoration and furnishing of the house was undertaken by one of England's most prestigious design companies in collaboration with an American designer who had worked with the owners on a previous project. The starting point was a visit to Nancy Lancaster's famous 1950s yellow drawing-room in Brook Street, in nearby Mayfair. Paint colours were identified, fabrics for curtains were chosen, and decisions were made about what furniture and artworks would come from America and what would be acquired in London. The look can be aptly described as 'country house come to town'. Old-fashioned prints are combined with checks and plains, while oriental carpets, fine antiques and blue-and-white porcelain signal a predilection for collecting; all these elements have been arranged so as to give the impression of a harmonious and evolved whole. The house instantly became a true English classic: understated, rich in detail and extremely comfortable.

96 Grand design

This fairytale castle near Antwerp in Belgium is renowned as the home
and former atelier of Belgium's most respected collector and dealer –
an expert in an extraordinarily diverse range of objects, from early
Egyptian sculpture to baroque furniture, from simple country tables
and chairs to contemporary art and sculpture. His love and knowledge
of architecture and restoration have attracted commissions for many
projects all over the world. Known simply as 'the castle', this house is
filled with glorious collections spanning many centuries and cultures.
The pure-white dining-room is used to display blue-and-white Ming
china recovered from a shipwreck. Light pours into the orangery
through elegant oval-topped windows, illuminating not only plants and
flowers but also a diverse mixture of furniture, pots and porcelain. Floor
materials are an important part of any interior, and here they include
ancient tiles, waxed timber boards and intricate parquet, softened and
enlivened by many interesting rugs. The library and study are evocative
of the eighteenth and nineteenth centuries; they are characterized by
cabinets of curiosities that are perfectly at ease with modern linen-
covered chairs and sofas. This is no period pastiche. A master of the
art of interior design has created a unique family home.

opulent

97 Applied art

This spectacular but idiosyncratic London home belongs to a highly creative woman who weaves and makes quilts, wall hangings, exotic clothes and jewellery. She and her husband travel the world collecting textiles, folk art, trimmings and all manner of decorative items, beads and buttons, many of which are later incorporated into exuberantly colourful artworks. In the nineteenth century the house was a tannery, but it has been transformed by the present owner into a kind of exhibition gallery. The dominant colours are those of India and Mexico – pink, yellow, purple, red and blue – and every surface is treated as a canvas on which to create a story. There is a shell grotto in the guest bathroom and mosaic work in a variety of materials. The side of the purple staircase is adorned with an array of coloured motifs, and even the floor and splashback in the kitchen have been decorated. Elsewhere there are paper montages, patterned ethnic rugs and collections of iconography. If the owner had not embraced her theme so wholeheartedly in every corner of the house, the result might have been chaotic, but instead she has created a gallery of applied decoration interspersed with just the odd plain piece.

opulent

opulent

98 Accent on black

The fabric and fashion designer who owns this Victorian villa in London satisfied her desire for a country-style space by adding an extension to the back of the house. A conservatory company built the L-shaped timber-and-glass structure, the walls of which are lined with vertical oak boards. Glass is a much more popular building material than it once was, now that technological advances have made it possible to provide good insulation in both the summer and the winter. One of the owner's most popular fabric designs was a black-and-white neoclassical collection, and black remains one of her favourite accent colours. She has used it in a variety of ways in the house, in particular to create strong graphic lines. In the living-room, mouldings are picked out in black, separating the red, yellow and grey sections of the walls. Large-scale artworks are hung symmetrically in black frames; the fireplace is black; and a sofa is covered in black velvet. The bold and original use of colour harmonizes well with a collection of Arts and Crafts oak furniture and with ceramics from the 1950s and 1960s. The bedroom is painted in shades of grey; the wooden bed is finished in gleaming black lacquer. All the fabrics are from the designer's own range.

99 Constant reinvention

Overlooking a leafy square in London's Pimlico, this flat is owned by
a Frenchwoman of many talents: a writer, designer and artist who is
passionate about design with a difference. There is relatively little here
that is made of wood; metal, used in a multitude of ways, is the owner's
favourite material. Dramatic barbed-wire spheres hang from the ceiling
in her workroom; iron café chairs and tables are seen in abundance; and
great spools of coloured wire are stacked in the entrance hall to form
unusual pillars. Lanterns, urns and chandeliers are industrial in style,
and silvery ball bearings are piled in dishes. Amid this seemingly
alienating collection of items is a fascinating mix of antique textiles, glass,
silver and mirrors, all set against walls painted in rich colours and lined
with numerous bookshelves. Groups of disparate objects form intriguing
vignettes on every surface. Apart from the cooking and bathing spaces,
the whole flat can be used for relaxing, entertaining and even sleeping.
The owner creates stages for living, regularly changing the colours
of the walls and the placement of furniture. The windows are free of
curtains, and at night candlelight illuminates this highly original interior.

opulent

100 Parisian masterpiece

It is rare to find decoration more opulent or refined than that of this eighteenth-century house in the Marais district of Paris. The man responsible for building this magnificent residence was the foremost designer of the Palace of Versailles, and it is hard to imagine how one might begin to furnish such vast, historic rooms in the twenty-first century. Fortunately, the present owner is a designer who not only is an expert on the period and style but also has been collecting rare and precious pieces of furniture, textiles, carpets and sculpture since he was a teenager. This is the dream home of a man renowned in France for his decorating skill and his talent for restoration and drama. Every room is filled with work by the great craftsmen of their day – amounting to an inventory that reads like a museum collection. The ceilings were painted by the best artists; there are seventeenth-century Gobelin tapestries and Savonnerie carpets originally commissioned for the Louvre by Louis XIV; the bed *à la polonaise* is by Georges Jacob, and there are desks by André Charles Boulle and Jean-Henri Riesener. Even the bathroom with its pair of seventeenth-century embroidered damask screens is fashioned to look like a small private salon. The whole is a monumental achievement.

opulent

opulent

Credits

1 Design: Abby Yozell unltd; 27 Drydock Avenue, 7th Floor, Boston, Massachusetts 02210; +1 617 345 0008; ayozell@aol.com. Feature originally produced by Amanda Harling.

2 Design: Gregory Tolaram.

3 Design: Jorge Villon. Feature originally produced by Sally Griffiths.

4 Design: Geoff Player and Michael Reeves.

5 Design: John Minshaw Designs; 17 Upper Wimpole Street, W1G 6LU; +44 (0)20 7486 5777; johnminshawdesigns.com.

6 Design: Emily Todhunter, Todhunter Earle Interiors; Chelsea Reach, 79–89 Lots Road, London SW10 0RN; +44 (0)20 7349 9999; todhunterearle.com.

7 Design: Candy & Candy; +44 (0)20 7594 4300; candyandcandy.com.

8 Design: Constanze von Unruh, Constanze Interior Projects; 81 Mount Ararat Road, Richmond, Surrey TW10 6PL; +44 (0)20 8948 5533; constanze.co.uk.

9 Design: Jean-Louis Raynaud and Kenyon Kramer, Décoration et Jardins; 3 Place des Trois Ormeaux, 13100 Aix-en-Provence; +33 (0)4 42 35 232.

10 Design: Anne Kyyrö Quinn; 2.06 OXO Tower Wharf, Bargehouse Street, London SE1 9PH; +44 (0)20 7021 0702; annekyyroquinn.com.

11 Interior design: Charlotte Crosland Interiors; charlottecrosland.com. Art: first page, bottom right: Works by Jonathan Delafield Cook. Feature originally produced by Amanda Harling.

12 Design: Gilly Holloway Design Associates; +44 (0)7779 625544; gillyholloway.com. Feature originally produced by Amanda Harling.

13 Design: Candy & Candy; +44 (0)20 7594 4300; candyandcandy.com.

14 Architect: Alfred French III. Interiors: Robin Lovell. Decoration: Albert Haman. Feature originally produced by Amanda Harling.

15 Robert Hirschhorn Antiques; +44 (0)20 7703 7443; hirschhornantiques.com.

16 Design: Candy & Candy; +44 (0)20 7594 4300; candyandcandy.com.

17 Design: Donna Aragi, Estilo; 87 High Street, Wimbledon Village, London SW19 5EG; +44 (0)20 8944 6868; donna.aragi@estiloliving.co.uk.

18 Design: Emily Todhunter, Todhunter Earle Interiors; Chelsea Reach, 79–89 Lots Road, London SW10 0RN; +44 (0)20 7349 9999; todhunterearle.com.

19 Design: Target Living; 6 Burnsall Street, London SW3 3ST; +44 (0)20 7351 7588; targetliving.com.

20 Design: Jean-Louis Raynaud and Kenyon Kramer, Décoration et Jardins; 3 Place des Trois Ormeaux, 13100 Aix-en-Provence; +33 (0)4 42 35 232.

21 Design: Sarah Vanrenen Design; Unit 8, 1927 Building, 2 Michael Road, London SW6 2AD; +44 (0)7778 354816.

22 Design: Candy & Candy; +44 (0)20 7594 4300; candyandcandy.com.

23 Design: Candy & Candy; +44 (0)20 7594 4300; candyandcandy.com.

24 Design: Dee Reynolds.

25 Design: Sarah Vanrenen Design; Unit 8, 1927 Building, 2 Michael Road, London SW6 2AD; +44 (0)7778 354816.

26 Design: Helen Ellery.

27 Design: Constantin von Haeften, Coconut Company; coconutcoantiques.com. Feature originally produced by Victoria Ahmadi.

28 Design: Glyn and Caroline Boyd Harte. Feature originally produced by Amanda Harling.

29 Design: Rodrigo de Azambuja, Sociedade Inglesa; Rua da Emenda 26, r/c, 1200-170 Lisbon; +351 (0)21 342 25 26; sociedadeinglesa.com.

30 Design: Wessel von Loringhoven, Casa Nova; Königsallee 30, D-40212 Düsseldorf; +49 (0)211 32 69 52. Art: (clockwise from top left) picture 1: red acrylic column by Herbert Hamak, work seen through doorway by Bill Beckley, picture above table by Antoni Tàpies; picture 2: work above on right by Sigmar Polke, work against bookshelves by Emil Schumacher; picture 3: black frame (around work on wall) by Robert Rauschenberg; second page, picture 2: dark picture seen through doorway by Galli; picture 3: photograph above bed by Thomas Ruf; picture 4: two posters above settle by Ludwig Hohlwein.

31 Design: Niels Hansen and Steffen Reimers, Marché Noir; +49 (0)40 27 88 22 72; marche-noir.de. Feature originally produced by Victoria Ahmadi.

32 Design: Sara May. Feature originally produced by Amanda Harling.

33 Design: Matthew and Miranda Eden.

34 Design: Anne Machin Architect; 1 West Garden Place, Kendal Street, London W2 2AQ; amadesign.co.uk.

35 Design: Alison Sloga, Garden Whisperer; alison@gardenwhisperer.com. Feature originally produced by Amanda Harling.

36 Design: Esther Fitzgerald Rare Textiles; 28 Church Row, London NW3 6UP; +44 (0)20 7431 3076; estherfitzgerald.com.

37 Design: Mr and Mrs Wolf. Feature originally produced by Victoria Ahmadi.

38 Design: Debbie Urquhart; debbieurquhart.com. Feature originally produced by Amanda Harling.

39 Design: John Stefanidis, John Stefanidis Design; johnstefanidis.com.

40 Design: Leif Pedersen and Fiona S. Graham; lamaisondelahalle.com. Feature originally produced by Amanda Harling.

41 Design: Shonda Warner. Feature originally produced by Sally Griffiths.

42 Design: Nick Etherington-Smith; Pomona House, New King's Road, London SW6 4SJ; +44 (0)20 7736 6586. Feature originally produced by Nerida Piggin.

43 Design: Elisabeth Cawi; +49 (0)40 27 68 80. Feature originally produced by Victoria Ahmadi.

44 Design: Mimmi O'Connell; 8 Eaton Square, London SW1W 9DB; +44 (0)20 7752 0474; mimmi.oconnell@googlemail.com.

45 Design: Monica Apponyi, MM Design; Redloh House, 2 Michael Road, London SW6 2AD; +44 (0)20 7751 0171; info@mm-design.co.uk. Feature originally produced by Amanda Harling.

46 Design: Alexandra Stoddard; alexandrastoddard.com. Feature originally produced by Amanda Harling.

47 Design: Lulu Guinness; luluguinness.com.

49 Design: Peter Leonard. Decoration: Laurence Isaacson; pariscommune.net. Feature originally produced by Sabine Wesemann.

50 Design: Birdie Fortescue; +44 (0)1206 337557; birdiefortescue.com.

51 Design: Avril Delahunt, Delahunt Designs; +33 (0)5 53 20 99 94; auvergnats1@aol.com. Feature originally produced by Amanda Harling.

52 Design: Inge Sprawson.

53 Design: William Thuillier; 14 Old Bond Street, London W1X 3DB; +44 (0)20 7499 0106; thuillart.com. Feature originally produced by Amanda Harling.

54 Design: Anne Fischer, Fischer Wohnen; +49 (0)25 25 95 21 10; fischer-wohnen.com. Feature originally produced by Victoria Ahmadi.

55 Design: Stephen and Luisella Barrow.

56 Design: Daniel Dufour; la-cabane-perchee.com. Feature originally produced by Sabine Wesemann.

57 Design: Hugo Grenville; hugogrenville.com. Feature originally produced by Amanda Harling.

58 Design: Annabel Beauchamp.

59 Design: Claire Farrow. Feature originally produced by Rose Hammick.

60 Design: Gerard Conway, Gerard Conway Designs; gerardconway@hotmail.co.uk.

61 Design: Konrad and Fiona Adamczewsky. Feature originally produced by Rose Hammick.

62 Design: Roland Lebevillon and Maurice Savinel.

63 Architecture: Harry Scott. Design: Sophie Ryder and Harry Scott. Art: second page: portrait above fireplace by Joseph Tonneau, animal sculpture by Sophie Ryder; third page: work seen through door by Francis Holl.

64 Design: Holger Stewen, Holger Stewen Interior Design; Calle de Santo Domingo 12, 07001 Palma, Mallorca; +34 (0)971 727016; holgerstewen.com. Feature originally produced by Amanda Harling.

65 Design: Jaine McCormack and Robert Barber. Feature originally produced by Mary Gilliatt.

66 Design: Pauline Mann.

67 Design: Julia Langton; +44 (0)1793 814950; burderop@ukonline.co.uk. Feature originally produced by Amanda Harling.

68 Design: Charlotte Smith. Feature originally produced by Sally Griffiths.

69 Design: Lesley Cooke, Lesley Cooke Design; lesley@chezcooke.com.

70 Design: Frederic Mechiche. Feature originally produced by Sally Griffiths.

72 Design: Simon Munn and Lesley Hall, Munn & Hall Associates; The Old Mill, Old Mill Lane, Sheet, Hampshire GU31 4DA; +44 (0)1730 268296. Feature originally produced by Amanda Harling.

73 Design: Sarah Featherstone, Featherstone Associates; 25 Links Yard, Spelman Street, London E1 5LX; +44 (0)20 7539 3686; featherstone-associates.co.uk.

74 Design: Dominic Ash, Dominic Ash Ltd; Manor Farm Outbuildings, Manor Farm, Compton Abdale, Gloucestershire GL54 4DP; +44 (0)1242 890184; dominicash.co.uk.

75 Design: Claire Bataille and Paul Ibens, Claire Bataille & Paul Ibens Design; bataille-ibens.be. Art: (clockwise from top left) picture 2: figure in alcove by Keith Haring; sculpture on shelf by Yves Klein; second page, picture 1: large work by Joseph Beuys. Feature originally produced by Sally Griffiths.

76 Design: Ernest de la Torre, De La Torre Design; delatorredesign.com. Art: (clockwise from top left) picture 2: work above fireplace Electric Chair by Andy Warhol; picture 3: bronze floor-standing sculpture by Henry Moore, work above sofa by Jean Dubuffet (1965); second page: work above fireplace Tête de Femme (1922) by Pablo Picasso; third page: silver gelatin photographs by McDermott & McGough; fourth page: work on stand by Antoni Tàpies.

77 Design: Michael Reeves; 30 Old Church Street, London SW3 5BY; +44 (0)20 7351 6515. Feature originally produced by Amanda Harling.

78 Design: Uschi Stuart.

79 Design: Luz Vargas, Luz Vargas Architects; luzvargas.com.

80 Design: Candy & Candy; +44 (0)20 7594 4300; candyandcandy.com.

81 Design: Ruth Aram, Aram Store; 110 Drury Lane, London WC2B 5SG; +44 (0)20 7557 7557; aram.co.uk.

82 Design: Wessel von Loringhoven, Casa Nova; Königsallee 30, D-40212 Düsseldorf; +49 (0)211 32 69 52.

83 Design: Ric and Deborah Ramswell, No Added Sugar; Unit 1, New North House, 202–208 New North Road, London N1 7BJ; +44 (0)20 7226 2323; noaddedsugar.co.uk. Feature originally produced by Amanda Harling.

84 Design: Aziz Cami and Grant White. Art: (clockwise from top left) picture 2: work on left of mirror by Andrew Johnstone; picture 3: work on right of mirror by Philip Mead; second page: work on left by Andrew Johnstone, work on right by Bridget Leaman; third page: five photographs by Brian Griffin; fourth page, picture 1: photograph by Brian Griffin; picture 4: photographs by (left to right) Elliott Erwitt, Henri Cartier-Bresson and George Zimbel. Feature originally produced by Sally Griffiths.

85 Design: Glyn Emrys, A-EM; CAP House, 9–12 Long Lane, London EC1A 9HA; a-em.com.

86 Design: Keith Skeel, Keith Skeel Antiques & Eccentricities; Loudham Hall, Pettistree, Woodbridge, Suffolk IP13 0NN; +44 (0)1728 745900; keithskeel.com. Feature originally produced by Amanda Harling.

87 Design: Brian Juhos; 35 Chelsea Crescent, Chelsea Harbour, London SW10 0XB; +44 (0)20 7795 0190; juhosuk@aol.com. Feature originally produced by Sally Griffiths.

88 Design: Isabelle de Borchgrave, Créations Isabelle de Borchgrave; +32 (0)2 648 53 50; isabelledeborchgrave.com. Feature originally produced by Sally Griffiths.

89 Design: Grady Cooley, Grady Cooley Interiors; 208 East 31 Street 2R, New York, NY 10016; gradycooley@hotmail.com.

90 Design: Freya Swaffer, Spencer Swaffer Antiques; 30 High Street, Arundel, West Sussex BN18 9AB; spencerswaffer.com.

91 Design: Giles Baker; theravengroup.co.uk.

92 Design: Michael Coorengel and Jean-Pierre Calvagrac, Coorengel & Calvagrac; rue de l'Echiquier 43, 75010 Paris; +33 (0)1 40 27 14 65; coorengel-calvagrac.com. Feature originally produced by Sally Griffiths.

93 Design: David Hare, David Hare Designs; +44 (0)20 7792 2373; davidharedesigns.co.uk. Feature originally produced by Sally Griffiths.

94 Design: Graham Carr, Graham Carr Fine Arts Ltd; The Studio, New Estate Yard, Oxenwood, Marlborough, Wiltshire SN8 3NQ; +44 (0)1264 731377. Feature originally produced by Sally Griffiths.

95 Design: Sybil Colefax and John Fowler; 39 Brook Street, London W1K 4JE; +44 (0)20 7493 2231.

96 Design: Axel Vervoordt; axel-vervoordt.com. Feature originally produced by Sally Griffiths.

97 Design: Lauren Shanley, Contemporary Textile Art; laurenshanley.co.uk.

98 Design: Sue Timney, Sue Timney Ltd; 331 Portobello Road, London W10 5SA; +44 (0)20 8969 5000; suetimney.com. Feature originally produced by Amanda Harling.

99 Design: Nathalie Hambro; fullofchic.com.

100 Design: Jacques Garcia, Décoration Jacques Garcia; 212 Rue de Rivoli, 75001 Paris; +33 (0)1 42 97 13 20; chateau@duchampdebataille.com. Feature originally produced by Sally Griffiths.

Acknowledgements

Andreas von Einsiedel would like to thank warmly the producers of the features and the many owners, designers and architects featured in this book.

Published by Merrell Publishers Limited

81 Southwark Street
London SE1 0HX

merrellpublishers.com

First published 2008
Paperback edition first published 2012

British Library Cataloguing-in-Publication Data:
Einsiedel, Andreas
More dream homes : 100 inspirational interiors
1.Interior decoration
I.Title II.Thornycroft, Johanna
747

ISBN: 978-1-8589-4575-0

Produced by Merrell Publishers Limited
Design concept by Martin Lovelock
Layout by Paul Shinn
Copy-edited by Henrietta Heald
Proof-read by Isabella McIntyre
Printed and bound in China

Front cover: project no. 5
Back cover: project no. 11
Frontispiece: project no. 15
Dedication: project no. 73
Introduction images: project nos. 40 and 92

Andreas von Einsiedel has specialized in interiors photography for the past twenty years. Based in London, he works internationally, and is particularly known for his work using only naturally available light. He is a regular contributor to the *World of Interiors*, *House & Garden*, *Architectural Digest* and other titles in the United States, Australia and Europe. He has photographed subjects for more than twenty books, including *Dream Homes* (2005), *Dream Homes Country* (2009) and *Dream Rooms* (2010), all published by Merrell.

Johanna Thornycroft is a freelance writer and journalist who regularly contributes design features to newspapers and interiors magazines worldwide. She has travelled extensively and spent long periods of time living in Africa and the Middle East. She is the author of several books, including *The Provençal House* (2003), *The Russian House* (2005), *Dream Homes* (2005), *Dream Homes Country* (2009) and *Dream Rooms* (2010), all photographed by Andreas von Einsiedel.

9 781858 945750